ADVANCE PRAISE

"Andy Fish's meticulously faithful illustrations and Steve Altes's disarming humor bring to life a more-fact-than-fiction adventure."

–LEWIS PINAULT
MIT alum and author of *Consulting Demons: Inside the Unscrupulous World of Global Corporate Consulting*

"All the geekworthy one-liners, Easter eggs, and knowledge bombs you'd expect, plus tons of humor, a bit of romance, plenty of heart, and dazzling illustrations."

–MELWHEEZY
host, *Geekly Podcast*

"*Geeks & Greeks* was a blast to read – it fused geek culture, MIT, and the magic of a hack gone right perfectly. Any true geek will love this graphic novel."

–CHARLES WACHTER
executive producer, *King of the Nerds*

"Mind-scorchingly mirthful! Who knew that the diabolically creative pranksters of MIT, those gestating geniuses of physics and engineering, could make the earth shake – with fear, laughter, and lust – when they put their 'big fat throbbing brains' to it? At last, the raw, kinky, wig-walloping wonder of these iconic hacks is revealed in a graphic novel so amped, so combustive, it'll fry your cranial circuits like a solar storm."

–ARTHUR PLOTNIK
author of *The Elements of Expression: Putting Thoughts Into Words*

"At its heart *Geeks & Greeks* is a love story, between Jim and Natalie sure, but also between Jim and his fellow students with MIT. How we loved to hate MIT, how terrifying some classes were, how much a real family our living group became. *Geeks & Greeks* brings it all back!"

–OLIVER SMOOT
MIT alum and unit of measurement namesake

"In his ample and interesting notes to *Geeks & Greeks* Steve Altes lists four rules of hacking: (1) be witty and finesseful, (2) make it hard to bring off, (3) hurt neither people nor property, (4) don't get caught. The first three are a perfect description of the work itself. Everything from the story line to the artwork to the coloration reflects the heartbeat of MIT: excellence. Just as everything in *Geeks* reflects the great affection its makers have for that astonishing institution. In short the *Geeks* team has accomplished something that is, indeed, witty, and hard to bring off. They have hacked the hack."

–SAMUEL JAY KEYSER
MIT professor emeritus and author of *Mens et Mania: T̶̶̶ ̶̶̶̶b̶ody Knows*

D1404547   OV -- 2016

"A gonzo-brilliant visual feast that reads like a blizzard of engrossing frenetic activity, offering an ethnographic deep-dive into MIT hacking and hazing subcultures. *Geeks & Greeks* combines the high-brow intelligence of *Good Will Hunting* with the rowdy frat antics of *Animal House* and the heart of *Dead Poets Society*. There is barely a moment to breathe as this roller coaster careens through the worlds of high-tech hazing, devilishly original pranks, and swaggering intellectual one-upmanship. Fish's masterful illustrations leap off the page with their inspired perspectives and vibrant colors."

–JON B. COOKE
editor, *Comic Book Artist* magazine

"Read *Geeks & Greeks* for its hot fusion of wit, narrative, and imagery. Awesomeness to the nth degree."

–KARL IAGNEMMA
MIT research scientist and author of *On the Nature of Human Romantic Interaction*

"*Geeks & Greeks* is a crackling insider look into the world of MIT fraternities. If you've ever wanted to peek behind the doors where young geniuses hack and haze, let whip-smart Steve Altes be your guide."

–DOTTIE ZICKLIN
MIT alum and co-creator of *Dharma & Greg* and *Caroline in the City*

"A graphic novel replete with action sequences might seem an odd medium for a tale about one of the brainiest places on Earth, but after a few pages I was hooked. With *Geeks & Greeks* Altes and Fish have achieved something remarkable – they have captured the energy and quirkiness that are the hallmarks of MIT... One of *Geeks'* most valuable contributions is to shine a spotlight on a quality not often associated with engineering. Memo to the world: MIT is a place with a profound and deeply intelligent sense of humor. Unless you're performing pediatric neurosurgery, stop whatever you're doing and read this book."

–LOUIS ALEXANDER
Director of Alumni Education, MIT (retired)

GEEKS & GREEKS

Steve Altes
Writer

Andy Fish
Penciler

Andy Fish
Inker

Andy Fish
Letterer

Andy Fish
Veronica Fish
Colorists

With additional inking by Brian Flint
and additional coloring by Sally Scott.

Relentless
GOAT
Productions

For rights information and bulk orders, please contact SteveAltes@gmail.com.

Cover design by Steve Altes.
Cover illustration by Victor Marcos.
MIT Great Dome vector art by Applemoment Studio.

Published by Relentless Goat Productions.
First edition: March 2016.

Library of Congress Cataloging-in-Publication Data

Altes, Steve.
  Geeks & Greeks / Steve Altes (writer) and Andy Fish (illustrator). —1st ed.
  p. cm.
  ISBN: 978-0-9963504-4-0
  1. Massachusetts Institute of Technology—Fiction. 2. College wit and humor.
  3. Graphic novels. I. Title.

Printed in the United States of America.

DEDICATED TO
MIT POLICE OFFICER
SEAN COLLIER
WHO GAVE HIS LIFE PROTECTING
THE MIT COMMUNITY 4/18/2013

DISCLAIMERS

Obligatory "don't try this at home" disclaimer
No matter how fun it might seem, please do not attempt to imitate any of the hacks you see in the book. You could be suspended, expelled, arrested, seriously injured, killed, or worse – vilified on social media for being unoriginal.

Obligatory "fictitious persons" disclaimer
This is a work of fiction. Names, characters, places, and events are either a product of the author's imagination or are used fictitiously, and any resemblance to actual persons (living or dead), institutions of higher learning, business establishments, locales, or incidents is entirely coincidental.

Disclaimer to "fictitious persons" disclaimer
Certain Kickstarter backers agreed to make cameo appearances in this work. Consider them actors playing a role and infer nothing about the actual people from the characters they portray in this graphic novel. That is, unless you want to infer something favorable about them. In that case, infer away.

FOREWORD

by Matthew Pearl
author of *The Technologists* (Random House, 2012)

To outsiders, MIT is as intimidating as it is intriguing. I think one of the reasons I wrote a novel about it was to give me a way into the inner sanctum after years of curiosity about it. But I will probably always get lost whenever I cut through the campus.

The old chestnut to "write what you know" is helpful but incomplete. Storytelling has always involved telling tales of the long ago, the far away, the imagined and imaginary. As Steve Altes points out in the preface, there has been a pattern of stories about MIT written by rubbernecking non-MIT folks (myself included). The more walled-off a place is, the more people on the other side of the wall wonder and then write about it. Some of this writing about MIT comes out of history and research, some come from what I call *mathploitation*, when English majors try to create characters out of mathematicians and scientists.

Geeks & Greeks is a welcome addition to the library of material about MIT. To start with, the format of a graphic novel is well suited to a setting that has so many iconic visuals associated with it. The zippy insider's take on the MIT experience, furthermore, gives us that hall pass so many of us wished we really had.

I spent a good deal of time wondering what the first hack – complex prank – was at MIT. As you enjoy *Geeks & Greeks*, Steve and Andy will have you wondering what elaborate hack is unfolding right now.

PREFACE

MIT is a place of intellect, imagination, and iconoclasm. These characteristics make it a rich setting for stories, both fiction and nonfiction. Consider MIT's three most notable appearances in the literary landscape in the last 20 years:

- *The Technologists*, the award-winning 2012 historical thriller set at post-Civil War MIT, written by Matthew Pearl, the gracious writer of our Foreword.

- *Bringing Down the House: The Inside Story of Six MIT Students Who Took Vegas for Millions*, the 2003 bestseller by Ben Mezrich about MIT's card-counting blackjack sharks that inspired the movie *21*.

- *Good Will Hunting*, the 1997 Oscar-winning screenplay by Matt Damon and Ben Affleck and subsequent Oscar-nominated film.

Besides their setting, these outstanding stories share something else... a crimson pedigree. All three were written by Harvard gents. True, Matt Damon didn't graduate from Harvard, but he spent four years there and was just 12 credits shy of graduation when he bailed. I think that qualifies him as a Harvard gent if not grad.

Must MIT always rely on Harvard to tell its tales? I hope not. And why are MIT stories always written by someone named Matt or Ben? That's kinda weird too.

Look, I get that Harvard has a pretty stellar reputation in the writing arena. Heck, they even have a comma named after them. But we MIT geeks can throw down linguistically too. Have you read *Active Vibration Isolation for Precision Space Structures* by Tupper Hyde '88? Its elegant yet provocative meditation on dual feedback control was enough to challenge my understanding of the human condition.

And let's not forget MIT Research Scientist Karl Iagnemma, who is one of America's top scientists and an acclaimed fiction writer. Here's a typical day for Karl:

8 a.m.	design a better Mars rover for NASA
11 a.m.	polish *Paris Review* Plimpton Prize
1 p.m.	star in PBS *NOVA* episode – subject: can you believe this man exists?
3 p.m.	option movie rights to short story collection *On the Nature of Human Romantic Interaction* to Brad Pitt

And that's just a typical day. Imagine what an *outstanding* day might be for him. Why he might even get mentioned in the preface of an overgrown comic book! Wouldn't that be something?

Unbelievable! I hear the guy just accomplished that too. There is just no limit to what MIT people can do!

INTRODUCTION

A few words on...

... "geek"

I view the word "geek" as a badge of honor, not an epithet. I'm clearly a huge geek and I suspect many readers of this graphic novel embrace the term as well. Being a geek just means you are highly enthusiastic about certain pursuits and have amassed a large body of knowledge about them – be it computers, math, movies, music, gaming, comics, or whatever. So whether you consider yourself a geek, nerd, intellectual badass, or shun labels altogether, please understand that I have nothing but the highest regard for people with prodigious intellects and unabashed enthusiams.

... hacking

According to the official MIT Gallery of Hacks:

> "The word hack at MIT usually refers to a clever, benign, and 'ethical' prank or practical joke, which is both challenging for the perpetrators and amusing to the MIT community (and sometimes even the rest of the world)."

> hacks.mit.edu

The Gallery defines "ethical" in the context of hacking:

> "According to the 'hacker ethic,' a hack must:
> - be safe
> - not damage anything
> - not damage anyone, either physically, mentally or emotionally
> - be funny, at least to most of the people who experience it"

> hacks.mit.edu/misc/ethics.html

Nightwork: A History of Hacks and Pranks at MIT by Institute Historian T. F. Peterson (MIT Press, 2011) elaborates on hacking motivations:

> "Before the term hacking became associated with computers, MIT undergraduates used it to describe any activity that took their minds off studying, suggested an unusual solution to a technical problem, or generally fostered nondestructive mischief. Hacks can be technical, physical, virtual, or verbal. Often the underlying motivation is to conquer the inaccessible and make possible the improbable. Hacks can express dissatisfaction with local culture or with administrative decisions, but mostly they are remarkably good-spirited."

... veracity

Since 100% of the events depicted in this graphic novel are not 100% true I must classify the work as fiction. Nevertheless much of this story was inspired by actual events that I, my friends, and fellow MIT students lived through. Yes, I've taken liberties. Timelines have been altered. Hacks that occurred decades apart in real life happen the same day in this story. And some incidents have been fabricated or embellished.

Have I taken creative license for the sake of the story? Absolutely. I'll be the first to acknowledge that some of these events did not occur. But you might be surprised to discover how many actually did.

... comprehensiveness

Hardcore MIT hack fans may bemoan the omission of their favorite. Even the Harvard-Yale football game weather balloon hack, MIT's greatest hack (as determined by the MIT Alumni Association's 2014 Hack Madness poll), doesn't appear in this tale.

To all such disappointed aficionados, I apologize in advance. To do justice to all the brilliant hacks MIT students have perpetrated over the years would require a novel the size of *Atlas Shrugged*. Plus I never intended to create a comprehensive encyclopedia of MIT hacks. There are several fine books on the subject already.

My goal was to tell the story of a unique time and place and pay homage to the most extraordinary group of geniuses I've ever known, told against the backdrop of MIT's quirky hacking culture.

... time warping

Techies are bug finders by nature, hardwired to find errors. Before you email me saying I goofed because MIT freshmen don't pledge fraternities, sororities, or independent living groups right away, please know that I realize that nowadays MIT students are required to live in dormitories their freshman year. However when I was a freshman in 1980, we rushed and pledged these organizations the first week of the semester, just as they do in this graphic novel.

Likewise, in this graphic novel the Quincy Quarries are still full of water, not dirt from Boston's "Big Dig" (Central Artery/Tunnel Project), because that's how things were when I was an MIT student. On the other hand, this story is clearly set in the present since it features things like smartphones and the MIT Stata Center, which weren't around in the 1980s.

Fire up the DeLorean, McFly! The time-space continuum is unraveling.

If you are knowledgeable enough about MIT or Boston to notice such temporal disconnects and they bother you, perhaps you can tell yourself this story takes place in an alternative universe MIT/Boston, where some things are the same as today, some things are the way they were in the past, and some things are a little bit different.

Or perhaps you could burn off that pent up fact-checking energy by searching for technical inaccuracies in *The Martian*.

... living groups
This story focuses on hacks perpetrated by fraternities. For the record, know that MIT dormitory residents are just as active in hacking as their Greek kinfolk, if not more so.

... identities
The names of MIT living groups have been changed to protect the guilty, with one notable exception. It's well known that Lambda Chi Alpha painted the Smoot markers on the Harvard Bridge. To pretend otherwise and change the name of that particular fraternity in connection with that particular hack seemed ridiculous.

The fraternity as the center of this story, Alpha Zeta Omicron, is fictional. There is no AZO fraternity at MIT, nor does it stand for any specific living group. AZO embodies both the excellence and excess I observed in MIT living groups – the daring hack-lovers who delight us with their ingenuity and irreverence, but sometimes take things a little too far.

... gender equity
Female characters are in short supply in this story despite MIT's male/female ratio being close to 50/50 today. Inescapable conclusion: I am a sexist pig.

Fun fact: not true. I couldn't be a bigger supporter of female engineers, female hackers, female you-name-its.

When I started at MIT it was still 80% male and there were no sororities. The events in this graphic novel largely reflect my actual experiences living in an MIT fraternity, dealing with a large group of guys with a penchant for pranks. In truth, the women I did know at MIT were far too levelheaded to be involved in many of the absurd events that are recounted in *Geeks & Greeks*.

... racism
Some reader or reviewer will undoubtedly accuse me of racism for creating "Ebony City," an exclusively African-American living group in this graphic novel. If doing such a thing is racist, it will surely come as a surprise to the residents of MIT's actual African-American living group, "Chocolate City."

... hazing
Certain events in this graphic novel are more akin to hazing than hacking. That was the reality of my experience at MIT and that's how it's portrayed in the story. It's a whole spectrum of collegiate and fraternal behavior, from the inspired to the idiotic.

To understand this story in its proper historical context, consider the evolution of MIT's position on hazing over the last 60 years.

2016

Today MIT has a strict anti-hazing policy – so strict that your average student would be hard-pressed to avoid running afoul of it at some point. Give someone the silent treatment, call him an obnoxious nickname, or practice a little deception, and you're hazing, Blutarsky.[1] Bystanders beware too – witnessing and failing to report such acts also constitutes hazing.

MIT campus life wasn't always this stringent.

1956

A little after midnight on February 10, 1956 MIT freshman Thomas Clark '59 was dropped off in a remote spot near the Waltham town line and told to find the way back to his fraternity as part of an initiation rite. Eight days later Clark's body was recovered at the bottom of the Cambridge Reservoir. Police theorize the teen mistook the ice-covered reservoir for an open meadow and fell through the thin ice.

In response to Clark's death, MIT President James R. Killian, Jr. said that MIT would "eliminate those excesses associated with hazings."[2] Note that he did not say the Institute would eliminate hazing, just its *excesses*.

Even the lad's father had a reaction that was remarkably forgiving by today's standards. Alfred Clark stated that he didn't blame MIT or the local fraternity for his son's death. "I blame the national officers of the fraternity. They are supposed to be more experienced and mature... the boys are inexperienced. Yet they are left to decide alone when a boy under initiation has reached the breaking point."[3]

The inference being it's okay to put pledges in onerous situations during initiation. Just don't push them past the breaking point. We are all products of our times. And in the 1950s the attitude was very much "boys will be boys."

1980s

Thirty years after the Clark case, hazing was still quite common in the MIT fraternity system. At the risk of sounding like a hazing apologist, I will say that in my era my fraternity never engaged in degrading or dangerous forms of hazing (i.e., eating goat entrails, coerced binge drinking) and only rarely practiced indiscriminate hazing ("because you are a freshman"). Rather it was predominantly hazing with a message ("because you did something the brotherhood would like to see less of").

For example, let's say Sam spends Saturday morning with his girlfriend at Wellesley instead of helping his pledge class pick up trash around the Charles River basin. His pledge class *could* leave a sternly-worded note on Sam's desk. But in their

---

1   MIT Hazing Policy, bit.ly/geeks-hazing

2   "Hazing Affair May Cut Frat Freedom," *Harvard Crimson*, March 2, 1956, bit.ly/geeks-killian

3   "MIT Undergraduate, Hazing Week Victim, Discovered Drowned," *Columbia Spectator*, February 20, 1956, bit.ly/geeks-clark

minds, the only acceptable solution is to deposit the giant bags of trash in the slacker's bed.

We viewed this sort of mild hazing as a form of social recalibration. Someone needed to have their priorities realigned or be reminded of their group obligations. And as long as it wasn't taken to extremes it was generally viewed light-heartedly by all concerned, hazee included.

No one was immune from hazing, not even seniors, although hazing was generally performed in a downward or lateral direction by class year. A sophomore better have an ironclad reason if he planned to haze a junior.

The more experienced hazing practitioners could elevate it to a form of performance art, done as much for the amusement of the brotherhood as for sending a message to a wayward pledge. And, as with hacks, hazing at MIT often involved a technical element, intricate planning, and a substantial degree of difficulty.

In my fraternity one pledge had the irritating habit of borrowing other people's furniture – swapping his own broken desk chair for someone else's perfectly fine chair, switching mattresses with someone. It was meant as a joke, but it went on too long and a line was crossed. One day he returned to the fraternity after class and discovered that all his furniture (bed, desk, lamps, chair, etc.) had been suspended in mid-air using ropes in the airshaft between our four-story Back Bay brownstone and the adjacent Boston University dorm. It looked like Spider-Man shot a giant web between the two buildings and tossed all the furniture out the window.

Poetic justice often played a part in hazing. Commit a furniture infraction and your furniture may pay the price. Shirk your kitchen duties and some form of food may make an unexpected and unwelcome appearance in your life.

One year a diabolical hazing innovator in my fraternity created the Dice of Doom – a dodecahedron with various MIT majors on each of its 12 sides. When someone earned the brotherhood's wrath, the Dice of Doom would be rolled. If it came up "Chemistry," then some sort of chemical reaction would play a part in the hazing. If "Ocean Engineering" came up, the Charles River might be involved. And so on.

Of course, things frequently got out of hand. The punishment sometimes exceeded the crime or the hazee would retaliate and spark a prank war, pitting one faction of the brotherhood against another. Or a hazing prank would miss its intended target, inflict collateral damage, and instigate a new feud.

Sometimes the hazing recipient was unjustly accused. Consider Sam from the earlier example. Maybe he wasn't absent-minded that Saturday morning, but was instead comforting his girlfriend who had just learned of a death in her family. Or maybe his bus broke down and he was stranded on the side of the road. When Sam returns to the fraternity and finds river refuse in his bed, he, in all likelihood, is going to go ballistic and exact revenge on those who hazed him. And around and around it went.

I don't think the MIT administration had any idea how prevalent hazing was in the fraternity system in this era. I doubt one percent of hazing incidents ever got reported to school officials.

1997
For the MIT community, the cold mackerel to the face came on September 29, 1997 when fraternity pledge Scott Krueger '01 died after forty hours in a coma. Cause of death: acute alcohol intoxication and aspiration. Or, to put it less clinically, he drank enough Bacardi rum to bring his blood-alcohol level to a toxic 0.4 then passed out and choked on his own vomit.[4]

Krueger did not die in vain. His shocking death convulsed MIT and led to sweeping reforms by MIT President Charles Vest. MIT freshmen were now required to live in dorms. Harsh penalties for underage alcohol consumption were enacted. Anti-hazing and alcohol education programs were implemented. And live-in graduate resident advisors are now a part of all MIT fraternities, sororities, and independent living groups.

The Krueger tragedy brought long-overdue attention to the problems of hazing and binge drinking at MIT. As a result of the changes I am confident that the next accidental death of an MIT student will not be due to alcohol.

Sadly, I have a pretty good hunch what *will* be the cause.

... falling
MIT students have a worrisome habit of rapidly transforming their bodies' potential energy into kinetic energy. Translation: they have a propensity for falling from high places.

I'm not talking about suicides. This plummeting problem is due to hacking gone awry and general carelessness.

August 24, 1993
An MIT junior fell three stories from an MIT dorm while rappelling with improper equipment.[5] He shattered his third lumbar vertebra and was in surgery for 14 hours.

February 16, 1997
An MIT senior fell four stories down the elevator shaft in his fraternity and was hospitalized for a week in serious condition.[6]

---

4   "Commonwealth's Statement of the Case," *The Tech*, September 25, 1998, bit.ly/geeks-krueger

5   "Student Hospitalized After 3-Story Fall," Jeremy Hylton, *The Tech*, August 26, 1993, bit.ly/geeks-fall

6   "LCA Brother Hospitalized," Tiffany Lin, *The Tech*, February 21, 1997, bit.ly/mit-lca

November 28, 1999

At 3:30 a.m. an MIT freshman was roof and tunnel hacking when she plunged 96 feet down the chimney of an MIT building.[7] A soot pile at the bottom of the shaft probably saved her life, but she needed 10 hours of surgery on her wrist and back.

January 29, 2006

At 2:30 a.m. an MIT freshman wound up in critical condition with numerous broken bones when she landed on a staircase platform after falling one and a half stories through a skylight on the roof of an MIT building while allegedly hacking.[8]

March 18, 2010

In the middle of the night an MIT freshman was exploring the roof access hatch in the 9th floor stairwell of an MIT building when he fell and seriously injured his legs.[9] He lay immobilized for hours until he was found by an MIT employee.

September 11, 2013

In an act that only Wile E. Coyote could appreciate, an MIT freshman jumped up and down on a fraternity rooftop skylight, which, not surprisingly, broke. He fell four stories and injured his head and genitals.[10]

There have been other incidents, but I think I've made my point.

Now consider the thorny position MIT is in with respect to hacking. On the one hand, hacks are an MIT tradition, a source of international publicity and recognition, a recruiting enticement to high school seniors, and a wellspring of student and alumni pride. On the other hand, hacking can be incredibly dangerous – students climbing on (often steeply curved) building roofs in the dark, maneuvering bulky equipment if the hack happens to be an installation.

My greatest fear for MIT is that someday a student will get killed while hacking. If that happens the student won't be the only casualty. Lawsuits and liability concerns could force MIT to abandon its longstanding tradition of embracing hacking, compounding the tragedy.

Future generations of MIT students, have fun but be careful. Make the most of your potential, not your potential energy.

---

7   "Freshman Injured in Fall from Rooftop," Matthew Palmer, *The Tech*, November 30, 1999, bit.ly/geeks-rooftop

8   "Freshman Falls Through Bldg. 5 Skylight," Angeline Wang, *The Tech*, February 1, 2006, bit.ly/geeks-skylight

9   "Student Fell, Lay for Hours at Stata Center," Michael McGraw-Herdeg, *The Tech*, March 19, 2010, bit.ly/geeks-stata

10 "MIT Student Seen Jumping on Skylight Before Fall, Police Say," Dan Adams and Martin Finucane, *Boston Globe*, September 12, 2013, bit.ly/seriously-wtf

"MIT celebrates hacker culture. Our admissions tours and first-year orientation salute a culture of creative disobedience where students are encouraged to explore secret corners of the campus, commit good-spirited acts of vandalism within informal but broadly – although not fully – understood rules, and resist restrictions that seem arbitrary or capricious. We attract students who are driven not just to be creative, but also to explore in ways that test boundaries and challenge positions of power."

Report to the President: MIT and the Prosecution of Aaron Swartz
(MIT, 2013)

"[A] hack is anything but a prank or tomfoolery. It goes far deeper than that. It is a kind of weapon in the hands of the MIT student..."

Prof. Samuel Jay Keyser
Mens et Mania: The MIT Nobody Knows (MIT Press, 2011)

PEPPERONI, MY ASS...

KOJI

CHIRP!

YOUR *MOVE,* GAIJIN.

GRIFFIN TO *UNICORN FOUR.*

DRAGON TO *VALKYRIE THREE.*

SAYONARA CHUMP!

CHECKMATE!

THREE IN A ROW FOR YOU.

THAT'S BECAUSE I POSESS A *COLLEGE-BOUND INTELLECT...*

...AND *YOU DO NOT.*

YEAH, WELL I DON'T HAVE A *HUNDRED GRAND* LYING AROUND.

MY SUBORDINATED DEBENTURES HAVEN'T MATURED YET.

NEITHER HAVE *YOU.*

I'VE *CHANGED* KOJI.

NO MORE PRANKS.

FOUND ANY COLLEGES WILLING TO LOOK AT YOU?

NAH.

THEY ALL KIND OF ZERO IN ON THAT *EXPULSION.*

REALLY HORKS UP YOUR PLAN TO BE THE FIRST MAN ON *MARS.*

HOW DO YOU KNOW I'M NOT ALREADY *THERE?*

STILL KNEE-DEEP IN SNOT-NOSED URCHINS?

THAT PLACE IS A *PETRI DISH!*

HOW DO YOU WAKE UP AND NOT COMMIT *HARA-KIRI?*

ASTRONAUTS NEVER GIVE UP, AND NEITHER DO I.

CHECK YOUR SIX! ANOTHER *HIDEOUS ALIEN!*

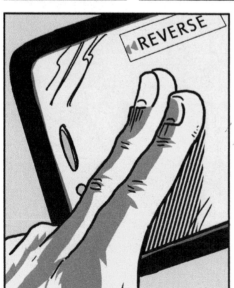

I DIDN'T KNOW YOU APPLIED TO *MIT.*

I DIDN'T.

"GREETINGS FROM MIT'S PROJECT SEARCHLIGHT... YADA, YADA... SEEKS TO NURTURE *INTELLECTUAL PRODIGIES.*"

ARE THEY TALKING ABOUT *ME?*

"...BLAH, BLAH... WE THEREFORE AWARD YOU...."

"...A *FULL-TUITION SCHOLARSHIP!*"

IT'S A *MIRACLE!*

DON'T BLOW THIS.

MOM, I'M DONE WITH *SHENANIGANS.* MIT IS *SERIOUS BUSINESS...*

...NOT A PLACE FOR *PRANKS.*

FOUR MONTHS LATER.

LOGAN INTERNATIONAL AIRPORT

ENTERING EST. 1630 BOSTON

NEED HELP?

ARRIVALS

NO, I ALWAYS STEAM CLEAN MY SHIRT WHILE I'M *WEARING* IT.

YOU KNOW WHAT YOU'RE DOIN'?

THAT DON'T LOOK *AAA* APPROVED.

ARE YOU FREAKIN' KIDDIN?

WHERE TO, *MACGYVER?*

CAMBRIDGE, MASSACHUSETTS.

"STUDENTS AND THOSE PASSING BY THE MIT CAMPUS ON MEMORIAL DRIVE IN CAMBRIDGE WOKE TO A SURPRISE THIS MORNING..."

"...FINDING WHAT APPEARED TO BE A CAMPUS POLICE CAR PARKED ON THE ROOF OF THE GREAT DOME."

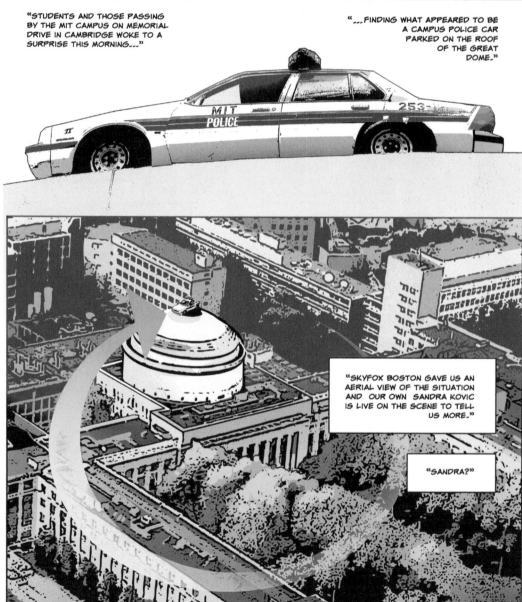

"SKYFOX BOSTON GAVE US AN AERIAL VIEW OF THE SITUATION AND OUR OWN SANDRA KOVIC IS LIVE ON THE SCENE TO TELL US MORE."

"SANDRA?"

28

HOW'D THEY *DO* THAT?

MY SOURCES TELL ME THEY GOT BODY PARTS FROM A CHEVY CAVALIER AT A JUNKYARD,

HAULED THEM UP THERE PIECE BY PIECE, AND ASSEMBLED IT ALL ON A WOODEN FRAME.

THE POLICE LIGHTS CAME FROM A FLEA MARKET.

SO I HEAR.

THINGS ALWAYS THIS CRAZY AROUND HERE?

PRETTY MUCH.

AND PULLING A BIG HACK ON THE FIRST DAY OF RUSH IS ONE WAY MIT FRATERNITIES AND DORMS COMPETE FOR FRESHMEN.

SO WHICH IS BEST?

DEPENDS.

YOU HAVE TIME FOR A RAPID-FIRE ETHNOGRAPHIC IMMERSION INTO MIT LIVING GROUP SUBCULTURES?

EACH FRATERNITY OR DORM HAS ITS OWN PERSONALITY.

SOME PRIDE THEMSELVES ON ATHLETICS.

"SOME EMPHASIZE *STUDENT GOVERNMENT*."

"AND THIS PLACE IS THE LEADING SUPPLIER OF *RECREATIONAL PHARMACEUTICALS* ON THE EAST COAST."

"BUT ALL LIVING GROUPS HAVE *ONE THING* IN COMMON...."

...A *PASSION* FOR HACKING. AND *NO ONE* TAKES THAT MORE SERIOUSLY THAN MY FRATERNITY, ALPHA ZETA OMICRON.

OFFICE OF THE DEAN

WHY?

I'LL SHOW YOU.

KABLAM!

BUT WE'VE GOT PLANS OF OUR **OWN!**

MEET LUKE BARDOLF, OUR RESIDENT NINJA.

JIM'S A FULL-RIDE FROSH WHO GOT PUNTED FROM HIGH SCHOOL FOR A PRANK.

DAZZLE ME.

"TO PAY FOR A TWENTY GRAND UPGRADE TO THE TEACHER'S LOUNGE, MY SCHOOL ELIMINATED THE COMPUTER LAB. THAT DIDN'T SIT WELL WITH ME, SO I BROUGHT THREE SMALL PIGS TO SCHOOL AND LET 'EM LOOSE."

THAT'S YOUR BIG PRANK?

"BEFORE I LET THE PORKERS GO, I PAINTED ONE, TWO, AND FOUR ON THEM. THEY GOT ROUNDED UP IN TEN MINUTES, BUT THE SCHOOL SPENT **ALL DAY** TRYING TO FIND PIGGY NUMBER THREE...."

"...WHICH DIDN'T **EXIST**."

THAT IS WOEFULLY LOW-TECH AND I'M NOT SURE *PETA* WOULD APPROVE.

I GOTTA GET MY GEAR FOR THE *HOTEL CAPER.*

LOOK WHAT GOT HIM THE SCHOLARSHIP.

BUT THE THING WITH THE NUMBERS DOES SHOW A *FAINT* GLIMMER OF CREATIVITY.

WHAT'S THE TRICK?

SOLVE THE VERTICES FIRST, THEN THE EDGES?

A MAGICIAN NEVER REVEALS HIS SECRETS.

INTERESTING CHOICE OF WORDS SINCE A MAGICIAN IS REALLY AN *ILLUSIONIST.*

WHAT ARE YOU DOING?

DELETING YOU SO I CAN ISOLATE ANYTHING ELSE THAT MOVES...

LIKE THAT *CLOCK.*

ZOOM

A-HA!

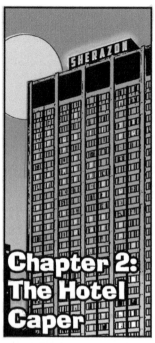

Chapter 2: The Hotel Caper

WHAT'S UP WITH ALL THE STATIES?

EVENING, GENTLEMEN.

"ABORT?"

"PROBABLY SHOULD, JIM, BUT THIS BLOODY TUX GIVES ME SO MUCH *CONFIDENCE.*"

WELCOME

MASSACHUSE
STATE
POLICE

TROOPER OF THE YEAR CEREMONY

BALLROOM A

THE 'N' ON THE ROOF IS OUT.

THANK YOU, BARTON.

HELLO.

WE'RE WITH MIT'S ALPHA ZETA OMICRON FRATERNITY.

WOULD YOU MIND TURNING OUT THE LIGHTS IN YOUR SIGN EXCEPT A, Z, AND O?

WITH RUSH STARTING TONIGHT, WE THOUGHT IT WOULD BE GOOD ADVERTISING.

I DON'T HAVE TIME FOR THIS, KID.

WE FIGURED YOU'D OBJECT, SO WE BROUGHT PROOF OF OUR RESOLVE.

THIS IS A GALVANIZED STEEL HEX NUT. YOU CAN FIND THEM MANY PLACES.

ESPECIALLY ON THE FUSE BOX AT THE BASE OF THE LETTER N ON YOUR ROOF.

NOW, WE COULD CLIMB BACK UP THE FIRE ESCAPE AND YANK THE REST OF THE FUSES. OR WE COULD DECIDE WE'RE TOO KNACKERED FOR ALL THAT AND TAKE OUT THE LIGHTS USING THESE HEX NUTS AS PROJECTILES FROM OUR *ROOFTOP FUNNELATOR.*

IT HAS A FOUR HUNDRED METER RANGE.

400M

39

A THIRD OPTION IS FOR YOU TO TURN THE LIGHTS OUT MANUALLY.

YOUR CALL.

THEY ARE HELIUM-ARGON LIGHTS, RIGHT?

ABOUT TEN GRAND A POP?

I'VE GOT A *BETTER* IDEA.

KOJI SAN

CALL

JIM-SAN

CHIRP!

THE HOTEL IS PLAYING HARDBALL. IMPLEMENT PLAN B.

SAY WHAT?

IN TEN SECONDS DIVERT ALL INCOMING TRAFFIC FROM THE HOTEL'S WEBSITE TO *MILFMANIA DOT NET.*

AND ON THE SPLASH PAGE BEFORE THE REDIRECT MAKE IT SAY, *"COURTESY OF FRONT DESK MANAGER JACK FLOREY."*

DAY ONE AND YOU'RE *ALREADY* PULLING A PRANK?

DOES NOT BODE WELL FOR YOU, DUDE.

WHOA!

BE *REASONABLE.*

DO WE HAVE A DEAL?

FIVE, FOUR, THREE...

YES! DON'T MESS WITH OUR WEBSITE.

HOLD THE REDIRECT.

JUST FOR *TONIGHT.*

THANKS, SPORT.

CAN YOU MAKE THEM BLINK TOO?

BY THE WAY, WHILE WE WERE UP THERE, I NOTICED THE A/C CONDENSER WAS SHAKING, SO I PUT SOME SHIMS IN AS A DAMPER.

CALL IT EVEN?

SLINK BACK TO THE DORMS, *NERD.* YOU'LL *NEVER* GET IN A FRAT.

AND YOU COULDN'T *COPULATE* EVEN IF YOU WERE A *HERMAPHRODITE.*

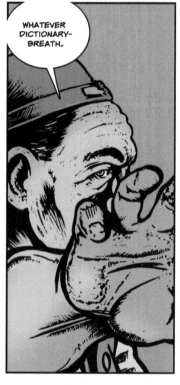

WHATEVER DICTIONARY-BREATH.

THIS ONE HOLDS *MUCH* PROMISE.

43

LATER.

WHAT'S THE DEAL WITH DEXTER?

YOU GUYS ARE RUSHING HIM HARD.

IS THIS A CRUEL PRANK?

WELCOME TO CASINO NIGHT

WON'T HE MAKE A FINE BROTHER?

YOU'RE KIDDING, RIGHT?

I'LL CONCEDE HE'S A TAD BOOKISH.

A TAD?

I ASKED HIM IF HE WANTED HIS DRINK ON THE ROCKS AND HE GAVE ME A LECTURE ON ARCHIMEDES' PRINCIPLE!

LOOK... WE WANT TO KICK ASS IN SPORTS...

...DOMINATE CAMPUS LIFE, THROW EPIC PARTIES, AND KEEP OUR GRADES IN THE STRATOSPHERE, RIGHT?

SO EACH YEAR WE RECRUIT NINE STUDS PLUS ONE GARGANTUAN GEEKAZOID. THEN WE MAKE HIM DO ALL THE PROBLEM SETS FOR HIS PLEDGE CLASS.

A MARVIN?

EACH CLASS HAS A MARVIN.

MARVIN WAS OUR FIRST INDENTURED HOMEWORK SERVANT. THE NAME STUCK. IT'S A SYMBIOTIC RELATIONSHIP. WE BESTOW SOCIAL LEGITIMACY ON THE MARVIN.

SO THAT'S DIABOLICAL.

HE PROVIDES US WITH AN IN-HOUSE NERD... A NERD ON TAP.

NEXT MORNING.

JIM WALDEN, DO YOU ACCEPT OUR BID?

I DO.

WE'RE NOT GETTING MARRIED, FRUIT LOOP. JUST SAY "YES" OR SOMETHING.

YES.

BRETHREN... YOUR PLEDGE CLASS.

WOO-HOO! FRESHMEAT! I MEAN FRESHMEN!

WOOT! WOOT!

PLEDGES, THIS SCAVENGER HUNT IS YOUR CHANCE TO GET TO KNOW BOSTON AND EACH OTHER. YOUR SCORES WILL DETERMINE YOUR ROOM ASSIGNMENTS,

SO IF YOU DON'T WANT A MOLDY, SPIDER-INFESTED CLOSET IN THE BASEMENT...

...I SUGGEST YOU DO YOUR BEST.

YOU HAVE ONE HUNDRED ITEMS TO COLLECT. PAIR UP, THEN MAKE LIKE THE RAIN FOREST AND VANISH!

HELP! I'M ALLERGIC TO MOLD, SPORES, ARACHNIDS --

RELAX! YOU AND I ARE A TEAM.

THE REAL QUESTION IS WHY YOU TECHIES WASTE TIME ON PRANKS--

--WHEN YOU COULD BE CURING CANCER?

I DON'T KNOW.

WHY STEAL A POLICE CAR INSTEAD OF DEVELOPING MORE EFFECTIVE BULLETPROOF VESTS?

I DON'T KNOW.

YOU CAN SPLIT AN ATOM BUT YOU CAN'T GET YOUR GLASSES FIXED.

WHAT IS IT WITH YOU GENIUSES?

I DON'T KNOW.

WHAT *DO* YOU KNOW?

I KNOW HOW TO SING "HAPPY BIRTHDAY" IN KLINGON.

I'M GOING TO PRETEND YOU DIDN'T JUST SAY THAT.

WELL, DON'T LET ME HOLD YOU BOYS UP.

I'M SURE YOU'VE HAVE KEGS TO STEAL AND COWS TO TIP.

INFERTILITY

EXI

... AND *ANOTHER* THING, I NEVER TIPPED A COW.

NOR I.

THOUGH I IMAGINE THEIR ELEVATED CENTER OF MASS WOULD FACILITATE THE TASK.

KENDALL SQUARE.

I FIND IT CURIOUS THAT NONE OF THE SQUARES IN CAMBRIDGE ARE ACTUALLY SQUARE.

KENDALL SQUARE IS A *TRIANGLE*, CENTRAL SQUARE IS A *TRAPEZOID* AND HARVARD SQUARE IS A *HYPERBOLA*.

IT TAKES A SQUARE TO KNOW ONE.

HOW'S YOUR DINOSAUR?

COME AGAIN?

ASK ANY PALEONTOLOGIST AND THEY'LL TELL YOU THAT BIRDS ARE THE DIRECT DESCENDANTS OF SMALL THEROPOD DINOSAURS.

SO THAT PIECE OF CHICKEN BREAST YOU JUST SWALLOWED IS REALLY A.... *DINOSAUR TIT-*

YOU MUST BE A RIOT ON A DATE.

SOMEDAY I HOPE TO TEST THAT HYPOTHESIS.

49

WHAT TIME IS IT?

PI O'CLOCK.

3:14

WE'LL MAKE IT IF WE RUN.

URCH!

SMOKING PROHIBITED

UH-OH.

IN FIRST PLACE, WITH THREE THOUSAND POINTS AND SEVENTY-TWO ITEMS... JIM AND DEXTER.

SPIDER CLOSET

HOWEVER, SINCE YOU RETURNED TWO MINUTES LATE, YOU ARE *DISQUALIFIED* AND WILL SPEND THE NEXT YEAR IN THE *SPIDER CLOSET*...

...*UNLESS* YOU REDEEM YOURSELVES.

WE'RE AT WAR WITH THE BETA KAPS OVER PARKING SPACES. YESTERDAY THOSE TROGLODYTES PUT A GARDEN HOSE IN HONDO'S JEEP AND FLOODED IT. YOUR MISSION IS *REVENGE*. YOU HAVE TEN MINUTES.

XMAS TUFF!

GO!

INTRODUCING THE H.P.W. OR HIGHLY-PRESSURIZED WATERMELON.

SPLAT!

FORTY-FIVE SECONDS!

"IN 1958 LAMBDA CHI PLEDGES USED OLIVER SMOOT'S BODY TO MEASURE THE BRIDGE..."

...AND TWICE A YEAR SINCE THEN, THOSE ROCKSTARS REPAINT THE SMOOT MARKERS.

THIS YEAR JIM IS GOING TO HELP US COME UP WITH A HACK JUST AS IMMORTAL. RIGHT, JIM?

SO I'M TOLD.

FIRST DAY OF CLASS.

RE-SMOOTIFICATION COMPLETE!

GET 'EM, B.T.!

WHAT'S HIS DEAL?

THE BRIDGE TROLL?

BEEN THERE FOREVER.

ONE OF THE GUYS WENT DOWN AND TALKED TO HIM ONCE. HE SAID HE'S PREPARING TO DEFEND EARTH FROM THE INVASION OF THE *EVIL SPACE REPTILES* FROM PLANET TEN.

OR SOME JIVE LIKE THAT.

DIE! DIE!

COURSE 8.01 – PHYSICS 1:
CLASSICAL MECHANICS
PROF. NEUSTADT.

ASSIGNMENT:
"WHACK NEWTON
BALL"

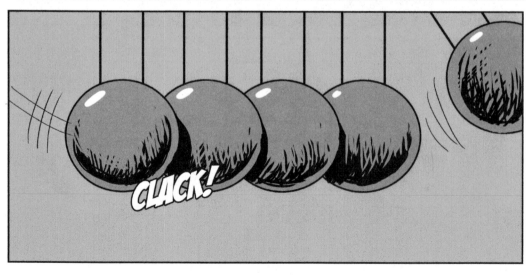

CLACK!

BE
GONE,
MISCREANTS!

WHACK!

MOTION...

TAK

PHYSICS IS THE STUDY OF MOTION, FROM GALAXIES TO BASEBALLS TO ATOMS.

IN MANY WAYS, PHYSICS IS THE ULTIMATE SCIENCE. BIOLOGY IS NOTHING MORE THAN GLORIFIED BUTTERFLY CHASING.

AND IF YOU CAN FOLLOW A RECIPE, YOU CAN DO CHEMISTRY. ONLY PHYSICS POSES MAN'S MOST *PRIMORDIAL QUESTIONS...*

WHAT ARE THE BUILDING BLOCKS OF MATTER?

WHAT IS THE ORIGIN OF THE UNIVERSE?

THERE IS BEAUTY IN PHYSICS, ONE THAT CAN ONLY BE APPRECIATED AFTER THE BEHOLDER HAS ACQUIRED THE NECESSARY TRAINING.

SOME OF YOU MAY GLIMPSE THAT BEAUTY AS WE UNCOVER WHAT MAKES NATURE TICK. WE BEGIN WITH NEWTON.

"CONSIDER A BALL IN MOTION..."

LATER.

LET'S GO, COEDS.

FIVE DOLLAR PITCHERS AT THE CASK.

RAINCHECK, LUKE. I'M UP TO MY ASS IN THERMO.

WE DIDN'T PLEDGE DEXTER FOR HIS LINEBACKING ABILITY.

YOU CAN'T FORCE DEXTER TO DO EVERYBODY'S PROBLEM SETS.

WHO'S FORCING?

SORRY DEX, O CHEM IS PROBABLY *TOO ADVANCED* FOR YOU.

WAIT....

I WAS ALMOST *DONE.*

I WOULD SAY THAT *PHENOL* IS MORE ACIDIC THAN CYCLOHEXANOL BECAUSE ITS CONJUGATE BASE IS STABILIZED BY *RESONANCE.* HA!

SEE? HOMEWORK IS *NERD CATNIP.*

SURE AND AFTER I GRADUATE, I'LL JUST CALL DEX EVERY TIME MY BOSS GIVES ME AN ASSIGNMENT I DON'T UNDERSTAND 'CAUSE I NEVER LEARNED THE FRIGGIN' MATERIAL.

DEX, DON'T LET THEM USE YOU OR YOU'LL END UP LIKE THESE MARVINS.

YEAH, DEX, DON'T BE SO *SPINELESS.*

I AM NOT AN *INVERTEBRATE!*

YOU TWO REBELS JUST EARNED A DATE WITH THE *DICE OF DOOM.*

THAT DOES NOT SOUND AUSPICIOUS.

THE NEXT DAY.

GENTLEMAN, I PRESENT THE GREATEST ADVANCE IN PLEDGE TRAINING SINCE THE PADDLE.

YOU MAY KNOW IT AS A HARMLESS DODECAHEDRON, A SOLID BOUNDED BY TWELVE EQUILATERAL PENTAGONS.

BUT IN *MY* HANDS, IT BECOMES...

THE DICE OF DOOM!

A TWELVE-SIDED DICE WITH MIT MAJORS ON ITS SIDES. WHEN A PLEDGE DISPLEASES US,

THIS SHALL DICTATE HIS *PUNISHMENT!*

TECHNICALLY, DICE IS PLURAL. IT SHOULD BE THE *DIE* OF DOOM.

64

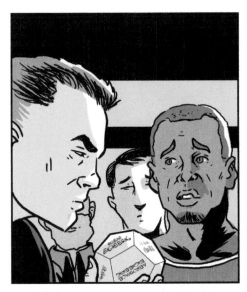

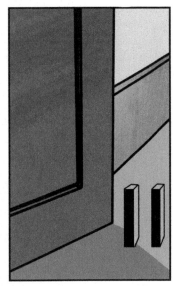

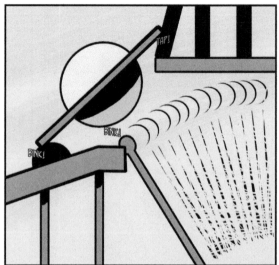

CRACKLE

THERE BETTER BE AN *ANTIDOTE!*

AT LEAST HE WASN'T STROKIN' IT.

COLLATERAL DAMAGE.

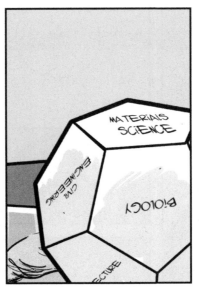

I HAVE FOOD FOR YOU.

WHAM!

OKAY, I'LL JUST LEAVE IT HERE.

INTRUDER!

CRAP!

WHAT DO I **KNOW?**

I KNOW THAT WITHOUT GEEKS YOUR CLIENTS WOULD BE DANCING AROUND A MAYPOLE INSTEAD OF USING IN-VITRO FERTILIZATION.

I KNOW THE TECHNICAL EXPLANATION FOR SOLAR ECLIPSES, DOUBLE RAINBOWS, AND THE GRAND CANYON, BUT I'M STILL AWESTRUCK WHEN I SEE THEM.

AND I KNOW YOU DIDN'T HAVE TO HELP US WITH THE SCAVENGER HUNT, BUT YOU DID ANYWAY,

SO THANK YOU.

I ALSO KNOW THAT THE ACETYLSALICYLIC ACID IN THIS ASPIRIN WILL MAKE YOUR FLOWERS LAST LONGER.

FLOP.

CAN I GET **HIS** SPERM?

THIS WEEKEND ALPHA RHO HIJACKED THE AUDIO AT BILL CLINTON'S SPEECH...

...AND CHANGED HIS INTRO MUSIC TO "I'M JUST A LOVE MACHINE."

THEN BETA TAU TURNED THE DOME INTO A GIANT BOOB...

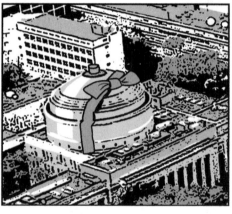

"...FOR BREAST CANCER AWARENESS MONTH."

IF WE DON'T DO SOMETHING ASS-SHATTERINGLY BOLD, IT'S GOODBYE GOLDEN DOME.

NATURALLY I HAVE A PLAN.

WE BUILD A MOCK-UP OF THE APOLLO LUNAR MODULE COMPLETE WITH O.J. SIMPSON MANNEQUIN AND PUT IT ON THE DOME.

IS HE... STABBING THE ASTRONAUTS?

IT'S AN HOMAGE TO "CAPRICORN ONE," CRETINS!

THAT'S PRETTY RAD, BUT INSTEAD OF PUTTING SOMETHING *ON* THE DOME, MAYBE WE PLANT SOMETHING *UNDER* IT.

UNLESS YOU'VE GOT A *PLAN* TO GO WITH THAT NEBULOUS IDEA, I SAY WE --

ACTUALLY, I DO.

"PARENT'S WEEKEND STARTS SATURDAY. AT NOON THE DEAN WILL LEAD PARENTS THROUGH THE MAIN LOBBY. SO I WAS THINKING WE AIM SOME LASERS...."

"...DEPLOY SOME TUNAGE...."

"... HANG AN INFLATABLE MYLAR DISCO BALL IN THE DOME SKYLIGHT...."

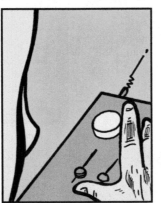

"...ADD SOME DRY ICE AND TURN LOBBY 7 INTO STUDIO 54."

GET DOWN, BOOGIE OOGIE OOGIE...

THAT HACK PRESENTS MYRIAD OPERATIONAL CHALLENGES

AND TWO DAYS IS NOT MUCH TIME TO PLAN.

HOWEVER... I LIKE IT.

SO WHO HANGS THE BALL?

AS ALWAYS, SUCH MATTERS WILL BE DECIDED BY *ZOLTAN*.

WWWWHHHIIIRRRR!

YOU ARE ZOLTAN'S ENEMY! YOU MUST BE DESTROYED!

YOU'RE SUPPOSED TO HELP ME, NOT UPSTAGE ME.

CLIK! CLIK! CLIK! ZZT! ZZT! ZZT!

THE INFINITE CORRIDOR, LADS. LONGEST STRAIGHT CORRIDOR IN THE WORLD. IT'S DIRECTLY ALIGNED EAST TO WEST,

SO TWICE A YEAR AT SUNSET, THE SUN SHINES ALL THE WAY DOWN, BATHING THE WHOLE CORRIDOR IN A GOLDEN BLAZE.

YOU A FREAKIN' TOUR GUIDE?

IT'S REALLY QUITE SPECTACULAR.

PROF. EDWIN PAULSON

PROF. ANDREW RALLIS

BAA!

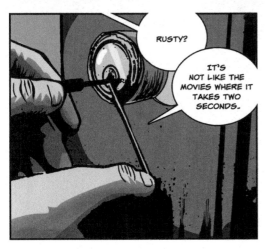

PROF.
PETER
FARRELL

CLICK!

DOME ACCESS
NO
ADMITTANCE

AT MY OLD JOB, WE DIDN'T HAVE KEYS FOR HALF THE VIDEO GAMES...

I GOT PRETTY HANDY WITH THESE.

REMEMBER, HACKING IS LIKE A ONE-NIGHT STAND.

GET IN, GET OUT, AND TRY NOT TO LEAVE ANYTHING THAT CAN BE TRACED BACK TO YOU.

WHOA....

CAN'T BACK OUT. ZOLTAN HAS SPOKEN.

I CAN'T BELIEVE I'M TAKING ORDERS FROM A *TOY ROBOT*.

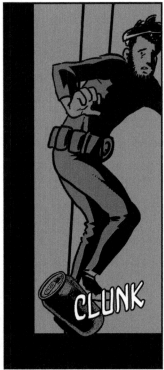

CLUNK

OOF!

HILARIOUS, GUYS!

ROPES SNAGGED AND WE HAVE COMPANY!

HANG TIGHT, JIM...

WHO'S IN THERE?

MAINTENANCE. GOT AN EMERGENCY WORK ORDER ON THE TRANSVERSE DOME VENTILATION DUCT...

THAT YOU, JONESY?

GOT NO TIME TO CHINWAG.

THERE'S A HINKY RHEOSTAT IN THIS A/C CONDUIT AND IF I DON'T REPLACE IT PRONTO, THE CENTER FOR ULTRACOLD ATOMS IS GONNA OVERHEAT AND WE'RE GONNA BE UP TO OUR ARSES IN HIGHLY AGITATED *QUANTUM FLUIDS.*

DIAL BACK THE BRIT SLANG!

NICE TRY, KID!

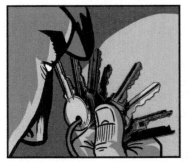

YOU BOYS ARE IN A WORLD OF TROUBLE. IT'S *DANGEROUS* UP HERE.

DOME ACCESS

NO

ADMITTANCE

WHAT THE HELL IS ON THAT ROPE?

IS THIS THE WAY TO BAKER HOUSE?

GET UP HERE! YOU COULD GET *KILLED.*

LET GO OF THE ROPE, SON. I GOT YA.

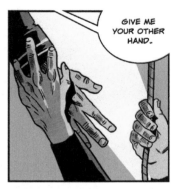

GIVE ME YOUR OTHER HAND.

GOOD THING WE DIDN'T USE THE LONG ROPE.

BACK-UP, LOBBY SEVEN. SEND EMTS.

HELP IS ON THE WAY.

RULE FOUR IS IN EFFECT.

"DON'T GET CAUGHT."

WE CAN'T.

HE'S DONE. DOES OUR GETTING COLLARED TOO HELP?

TEMPUS FUGIT.

HE'S RIGHT. MAKE LIKE AN AMOEBA...

... AND SPLIT.

MISTER WALDEN, IF YOU DON'T GIVE US THE NAMES OF YOUR ACCOMPLICES,

YOU WILL BEAR FULL **RESPONSIBILITY** FOR THIS **ACT OF VANDALISM**.

Chapter 4: Goneril and the Beaver Lover

PROF BRAD FELD

PRO

PROF LAMBEAU

OKAY.

THE OTHER GUYS WERE ARCHIE LEACH, CHARLES MARTEL, GENE CERNAN, AND AL DESALVO.

POINT OF ORDER.

NOW WE'RE GETTING SOMEWHERE.

YES, PROFESSOR NEUSTADT?

I BELIEVE THE ACCUSED HAS JUST IMPLICATED CARY GRANT, CHARLEMAGNE'S GRANDFATHER,

THE LAST MAN TO WALK ON THE MOON, AND THE BOSTON STRANGLER.

THIS IS **NONSENSE!** YOU WANT FULL RESPONSIBILITY?

FINE.

I'M GIVING YOU PROBATION. ONE MORE SLIP UP AND YOU'RE **OUT.** PLUS YOU NEED TO PAY RESTITUTION.

FOUR THOUSAND DOLLARS, DUE IN ONE MONTH. **NO** EXTENSIONS.

HEARING ADJOURNED!

BANG!

MEET ME IN MY LAB TOMORROW AT FIVE. ASSUMING YOU CAN REFRAIN FROM BEING EXPELLED THAT LONG.

AMAZING STUFF, THAT DUCT TAPE.

DID YOU KNOW IT HELPED SAVE THE APOLLO 13 ASTRONAUTS?

AND BEN HUR WON THE CHARIOT RACE. TELL ME SOMETHING I DON'T KNOW.

ANTI-MATTER WAS DISCOVERED IN 1933.

WHAT'S A GOOD WAY TO MAKE FAST MONEY AROUND HERE?

BIO-WHORING.

HUH?

RIP!

MEDICAL STUDIES.

DEAD TREE FLYERS

EARN BIG $$$

Earn $100 per WEEK!

Requires Multiple Rectal Exams Performed by Med Students

$200

al Tap Required

be available for ow up visits commitment

TUDENTS!! MONEY? T FAST!

TION MEETING l 14 at 4pm tel Cambridge d Square

e pizza

TAKE $50

978-555-0199

MIT MEN!

CHILDLESS COUPLES GROW THEIR FAMILIES!

LTH CHECK N & SANITARY FACILITY NAL MEDICAL ENVIRONMENT ONS PRIVATE

$150 PER NATION

TY CLINIC lls 02138

DONORS CALL TODAY 555-0100

MIT MEN

HELP CHILDLESS COUPLES GRO THEIR FAMILIES!

FREE HEALTH CHECK
SAFE CLEAN & SANITARY FACILITY
PROFESSIONAL MEDICAL ENVIRONMENT
ALL DONATIONS PRIVATE

$150 PER DONATION

CAMBRIDGE FERTILITY CLINIC
1841 Emerson St.
Cambridge, MA 02139

$150? I NEVER REALIZED SPERM WAS SUCH A *VALUABLE* COMMODITY.

I GOT A FRIEND BACK HOME WITH A TUBE SOCK THAT'S PROBABLY WORTH A QUARTER MILL.

CHARMING.

IF YOU WANT TO STOP BY THE DAY AFTER TOMORROW, WE'LL HAVE RESULTS FROM THE SCREENING TESTS.

BY THE WAY, I'M JIM.

NATALIE. AND I'LL PASS. I KNOW WHERE THAT HAND'S BEEN.

LOOKS LIKE JIM HAS A PET.

I LIKE YOU, TOO, TROLL.

YOU WANTED TO SEE ME, PROFESSOR NEUSTADT?

COME IN, MISTER WALDEN.

MIT HACKS ARE KNOWN FOR THEIR ORIGINALITY, HUMOR, TECHNICAL BRILLIANCE, AND ABOVE ALL,...

...BENIGN INTENT.

NOT A RECKLESS DISREGARD FOR LIFE AND PROPERTY.

UNDERSTOOD.

HOW'S RESTITUTION GOING?

IT'S A LOT TO RAISE IN FOUR WEEKS.

WOULD YOU LIKE TO WORK FOR ME?

REALLY?

I COULD USE A LAB ASSISTANT.

AND, I MUST ADMIT, I RATHER ENJOYED THE WAY YOU PARRIED THE CHAIRMAN'S QUESTIONS.

HE'S BEEN *INSUFFERABLE* SINCE HE WON THAT NOBEL PRIZE.

DEAL.

SPLENDID. LET'S GET STARTED.

UH... PROFESSOR NEUSTADT?

DON'T *MOVE.*

CLICK!

JESUS!

PFFT!

BANG!

CLICK!

HIGH-SPEED STROBOSCOPIC PHOTOGRAPHY,

ILLUMINATING THAT WHICH IS IMPERCEPTIBLE TO THE HUMAN EYE.

MY PASSION.

THE BOSTON GLOBE
SATURDAY JULY 6, 1974

MIT BUILDING BECOMES GIANT SOUND METER
Prank Surprises Pops Concert, Sets World Record

THIS WAS YOUR DOING?

I WAS IN GRAD SCHOOL.

IT WAS THE FOURTH OF JULY.

THE BOSTON POPS WERE PLAYING ON THE ESPLANADE AND YOU COULD HEAR IT OVER HERE.

TO GARNER A YOUNG LADY'S AFFECTIONS, I RIGGED THE GREEN BUILDING'S LIGHTS TO TURN ON AND OFF, RISING AND FALLING IN SYNC WITH THE SOUSA MARCHES LIKE A SOUND METER.

NEVER TOOK YOU FOR THE TYPE.

NOT EVERYTHING IS PERCEPTIBLE TO THE HUMAN EYE.

WE'LL CALL YOU AS SOON AS WE FIND A SUITABLE DONOR.

YOU PASSED.

WHAT MADE YOU DECIDE TO BE A DONOR ANYWAY?

HACK WENT SOUTH.... BUILDING DESTROYED....

RESTITUTION REQUIRED.

WHO WOULD HAVE *THOUGHT* A DESTRUCTIVE, CHILDISH PRANK WOULD HAVE NEGATIVE REPERCUSSIONS?

WELL, THE ENGINEERING INVOLVED WAS FAR BEYOND WHAT A CHILD COULD DO.

SO.... WHAT SORT OF TESTS DO YOU DO?

SPERM COUNT, MOTILITY, CHECK FOR HIV, STDS....

YOU DO ALL THAT HERE?

YEP. WOULD YOU LIKE TO SEE HOW?

I'M CAUTIOUSLY INTRIGUED.

PUNGENT BOUQUET... BOLD, YOUTHFUL. A HINT OF CHLORINE.

BIT OF A SALTY FINISH.

PASS.

YOU'VE SCARRED MY RETINAS.

TRY SOME.

I'VE GOT A BETTER IDEA.

HOW ABOUT WE GO FOR SOME PERUVIAN FOOD?

THERE'S A PLACE UP THE STREET.

MISSION STATEMENT

We pledge to do
we can to he
create the fam
dreams. And
your baby c
with a tail or
we swear it
to do with
qu
R

I'VE NEVER BEEN THERE AND I HAVE NO IDEA WHAT THEY EAT IN PERU, BUT I'M REASONABLY SURE IT'S NOT, YOU KNOW, INSECTS.

SO, YOU AND ME... DINNER... MAY OR MAY NOT CONSIST OF BUGS.

YOU MIT GUYS ARE SMOOTH.

I ALREADY HAVE PLANS FOR TONIGHT.

BUT YOU CAN WALK ME HOME.

...THE NOSE CONE SEPARATED, THE PARACHUTE DEPLOYED, AND JASPER FLOATED BACK TO EARTH,

WHERE HE RECEIVED A HERO'S WELCOME OF SUNFLOWER SEEDS.

OF COURSE, MY SISTER NEVER LET ME NEAR HER GERBILS AGAIN.

DID YOU ALWAYS WANT TO BE AN ASTRONAUT?

I COULD NEVER IMAGINE A GREATER ADVENTURE. AND IT MAY SOUND STRANGE, BUT ENGINEERS GIVE ME HOPE FOR THE PLANET.

LOOK... A *BEAVER*, NATURE'S ENGINEER. THAT LITTLE DUDE IS TRYING TO DAM THE CHARLES.

THAT'S WHY I LIKE ENGINEERS. THEY HAVE THIS INHERENT OPTIMISM. THEY THINK ANY PROBLEM CAN BE SOLVED WITH A LITTLE EFFORT.

THIS BEAVER FIGURES WITH ENOUGH TIME AND ENOUGH LOGS, HE CAN BUILD THE GREATEST DAM IN BEAVER HISTORY.

HE MAY BE A STARRY-EYED DREAMER TO YOU,

BUT TO THE REST OF US HE'S A BUCK-TOOTH PAIN IN THE ASS WHO'S CHOPPING DOWN BEAUTIFUL ELM TREES.

THIS ADMIRATION SIR, IS MUCH OF THE SAVOR OF OTHER YOUR NEW PRANKS.

HERE DO YOU KEEP 100 KNIGHTS AND SQUIRES,

MEN SO DISORDERED, SO DEBOSHED, AND BOLD, THAT THIS OUR COURT....

....INFECTED WITH THIER MANNERS SHOWS LIKE A RIOTOUS INN.

EPICURUSM AND LUST MAKES IT MORE LIKE A TAVERN OR BROTHEL THAN A GRACED PALACE.

THE SHAME ITSELF DOTH SPEAK FOR INSTANT REMEDY.

THAT WAS *RIDICULOUSLY GREAT!* NO.... THAT TAKES GREAT AND THROWS IT ON THE GROUND AND STOMPS ON IT.

PLUS IT WAS AN AMAZINGLY ACCURATE DESCRIPTION OF FRATERNITY LIFE.

I THOUGHT IT MIGHT BE APROPOS. HOW CAN YOU LIVE WITH THAT MANY GUYS?

I GREW UP WITH THREE SISTERS. MY LITTLE SISTER MADE ME ATTEND SO MANY *TEA PARTIES*, IT'S NO WONDER I ENDED UP IN *BOSTON!*

I ALWAYS WANTED A BROTHER. NOW I HAVE FORTY.

END OF THE LINE, YOU.... *BEAVER LOVER.*

A HANDSHAKE? PROGRESS.

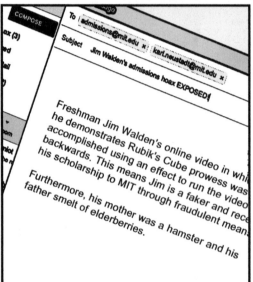

97

A *PLANETARIUM?* IS THIS A DATE OR A *FIELD TRIP?*

DO YOU KNOW WHY I'M INTERESTED IN THE MOONS OF *URANUS?*

BECAUSE YOU WATCH TOO MUCH "SOUTH PARK?"

BECAUSE MOST ARE NAMED AFTER *SHAKESPEAREAN* CHARACTERS.

THIS MOON IS CORDELIA, NAMED FOR THE SISTER OF GONERIL FROM YOUR MONOLOGUE.

THEN THERE'S THIS MIX OF INTERSTELLAR GAS AND DUST CLOUDS CALLED EMISSION NEBULA I.C. 1805, A.K.A. THE HEART NEBULA.

OOH, THE *HEART* NEBULA?

IS THIS HOW A GEEK GETS ROMANTIC?

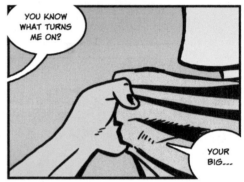

Chapter 5: Ratsicle Revenge

I GOT SPANKED BY THAT PHYSICS TEST.

YOU'RE THE ONLY PLEDGE WHOSE HOUSE DUTY ISN'T FINISHED.

SCHUBERT'S EIGHTH SYMPHONY WASN'T FINISHED EITHER. MANY CONSIDER IT HIS *GREATEST* WORK.

I'LL GET IT DONE. IT'S JUST THAT PROBLEM SETS TAKE LONGER WHEN YOU DO THEM YOURSELF.

WE PROVIDE A MARVIN. IT'S NOT MY FAULT YOU DON'T USE HIM.

NO OFFENSE, DEXTER.

⚡ KOFF ⚡ NONE TAKEN.

NOT ONLY THAT, I'VE GOT A JOB WITH PROFESSOR NEUSTADT --

REALLY? 'CAUSE IT LOOKS TO ME LIKE YOU'RE SPENDING A LOT OF TIME WITH THAT TANGY BRUNETTE.

I CAN'T HAVE A GIRLFRIEND?

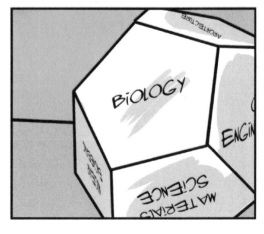

YOU'LL WANT TO USE THE DISCHARGE TOOL BEFORE REMOVING THE --

RELAX.

I'VE DONE THIS A THOUSAND TIMES.

ZAP!

MAYBE NOT WITH A CAPACITOR *THIS* BIG.

YOU THINK HACKS ARE SUCH A BIG PART OF THIS PLACE JUST TO WIN THE GOLDEN DOME?

Miami Institute of Technology

NOT ENTIRELY.

I THINK ENGINEERS LIKE A CHALLENGE AND OFTEN POSSESS A PARTICULAR SENSE OF HUMOR, A KIND OF CIVIL DISOBEDIENCE. SOMETIMES A HACK CAN SEND A MESSAGE, LIKE A POLITICAL CARTOON.

ARE YOU TELLING ME THERE'S A *MESSAGE* IN THOSE PINK FLAMINGOS?

POSSIBLY. IF SO, WHAT MIGHT IT BE?

WELL, FLAMINGOS ARE VERY COLORFUL.

UNLIKE THIS PLACE.

UNLESS YOU CONSIDER GRAY A COLOR.

SO MAYBE THE PERPETRATORS WERE SAYING, "HEY MIT, A LITTLE COLOR WON'T KILL YA."

INDEED.

THEN AGAIN, PERHAPS THERE IS NO MESSAGE.

THE IMPORTANT THING IS IT GOT YOU THINKING. YOU SAW THE WORLD A LITTLE DIFFERENTLY.

A HACK CAN ALSO DETHRONE AUTHORITY.

DETHRONE *AUTHORITY?*

ALLOW ME TO DEMONSTRATE. HAVE A SEAT.

THE MOST PRIMITIVE PRANK OF ALL...

...PULLING THE CHAIR AWAY AS SOMEONE SITS. THE PERSON GOES FROM BEING A FIGURE OF AUTHORITY

TO JUST ANOTHER LUMP OF MATTER, SUBJECT TO THE IMMUTABLE LAW OF GRAVITY.

IT ALWAYS COMES BACK TO *PHYSICS* WITH YOU, DOESN'T IT?

MY HALLOWEEN COSTUME!

DEXTER GARFINKEL
ALPHA ZETA OMICRON
BEACON ST
MA 02215

GNARLY LOOKIN' *SLEESTAK!*

IT'S THE *GORN* FROM STAR TREK.

JUST MESSIN' WITH YA. I KNOW A GORN WHEN I SEE ONE.

RELAX. IT'S ME, YOUR FRIEND.

FRIEND?

YOU *KNOW* HIM?

RO-A-A-A-A-R!

OH NO.

SPACE REPTILE!

WHO'S YOUR FRIEND?

DON'T KNOW HIS NAME. EVERYONE CALLS HIM THE BRIDGE TROLL.

WHAT'S HIS DEAL?

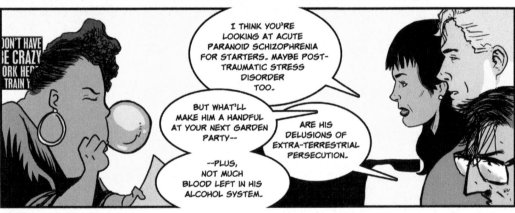

I THINK YOU'RE LOOKING AT ACUTE PARANOID SCHIZOPHRENIA FOR STARTERS. MAYBE POST-TRAUMATIC STRESS DISORDER TOO.

BUT WHAT'LL MAKE HIM A HANDFUL AT YOUR NEXT GARDEN PARTY--

ARE HIS DELUSIONS OF EXTRA-TERRESTRIAL PERSECUTION.

--PLUS, NOT MUCH BLOOD LEFT IN HIS ALCOHOL SYSTEM.

PLEASURE SERVING WITH YOU, CAPTAIN.

HOPE TO SEE YOU BACK ON EARTH SOON. THIRD PLANET FROM THE SUN. YOU CAN'T MISS IT.

SPACE REPTILE, I PRESUME?

ONE HOUR LATER.

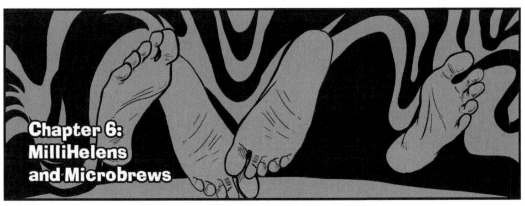

Chapter 6: MilliHelens and Microbrews

WHERE DID YOU LEARN *THAT?*

I LIKE TO TINKER.

YOU GEEKS HAVE YOUR ADVANTAGES.

SO HOW MANY MORE DONATIONS BEFORE YOU'RE OUT OF DEBT?

ENOUGH TO START A PRESCHOOL.

WANT TO EARN A LOT MORE?

HOW?

THE CLINIC IS DESPERATE FOR AFRICAN-AMERICAN DONORS.

WE'LL PAY YOU FIVE HUNDRED BUCKS FOR EVERY ONE YOU RECRUIT.

CAN'T BE SOME RANDOM GUY OFF THE T THOUGH. THEY WANT MIT OR HARVARD ONLY.

YOU WANT ME TO BE A... *SPERM BOUNTY HUNTER?*

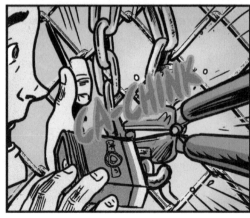

IT'S A UNIT OF BEAUTY. HELEN OF TROY'S FACE LAUNCHED A THOUSAND SHIPS,

SO A *MILLIHELEN* IS A FACE THAT COULD LAUNCH *ONE SHIP*.

I SEE. WELL, THIS IS A *MICROBREW*.

AND YOU'RE GOING TO WEAR ONE EVERY TIME YOU MAKE A COMMENT THAT DORKY.

GERONIMO!

SPLASH!

119

THIS CLIFF IS ONE HUNDRED FEET HIGH.

HOW DO YOU KNOW?

HONDO'S DESCENT TOOK TWO POINT FIVE SECONDS. THE DISTANCE TRAVELED BY A FALLING OBJECT IS ONE-HALF "G" T-SQUARED.

I GUESS NEWTON HAS HIS USES AFTER ALL.

SITTING BULL!

UNUSUAL PLACE FOR LOGGING.

NAH, MAN. THE CITY GOT SO TIRED OF SENDING CRUISERS OVER HERE THAT THEY TRIED TO CREATE A NATURAL BARRIER ON THE WATER.

THEY HACKED DOWN AN ACRE AND THREW THE LOGS IN THE QUARRY. THE MORONS THOUGHT THEY WOULD FLOAT.

GATHER AROUND, PEOPLE! I HAVE LIFE-ALTERING NEWS ABOUT ONE OF OUR PLEDGES.

WOO HOO!

GIRL POWER! JUMP WUSSES!

STOP JUMPING! DEXTER THINKS THERE'S LOGS FLOATING UNDERWATER!

REALLY? LET'S FIND OUT.

A-A-A-A-A-A-H!

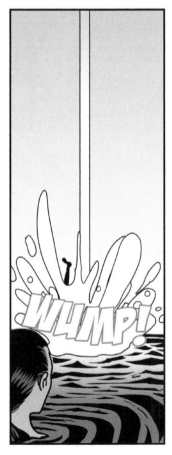

125

YOU'RE GONNA BE ALRIGHT, DEX.

KOFF

LUKE, THAT WAS AN INCREDIBLY **ASSHOLIC** THING TO DO.

SQUELCH IT, PLEDGE. IT WAS AN **ACCIDENT.**

NO, IT **WASN'T!** I TOLD YOU TO **WAIT!**

LOOK, WE'RE ALL IMPRESSED WITH YOUR HEROICS,

BUT IF YOU DON'T COOL IT I'M GONNA HAZE YOU BACK TO THE **PALEOLITHIC ERA.**

THEN THERE'S THIS CHECK STUB FROM A SPERM BANK.

APPARENTLY JIM IS SOME SORT OF *SPERM GIGOLO* AND THIS YOUNG LADY IS HIS *PIMP!*

YOU'RE *DISGUSTING.*

YOU'RE GOING THROUGH MY DESK? WHAT THE *HELL?*

WE'LL SORT OUT THIS PLETHORA OF BIZARRENESS BACK AT THE HOUSE,

BUT FOR NOW, ANYONE WHO DOESN'T WANT A HUNDRED DOLLAR TICKET FOR TRESPASSING SHOULD *BOLT.*

WEEEEEOOOOOO

NATALIE, I CAN EXPLAIN --

DON'T. YOU AND YOUR FRIENDS ARE *SICK.*

WEEEEEOOOOOO

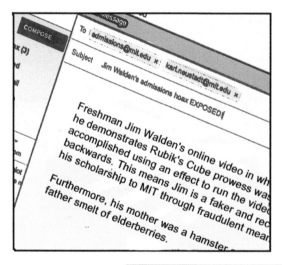

To admissions@mit.edu × | karl.neustadt@mit.edu ×

Subject   Jim Walden's admissions hoax EXPOSED!

Freshman Jim Walden's online video in wh he demonstrates Rubik's Cube prowess was accomplished using an effect to run the vide backwards. This means Jim is a faker and rec his scholarship to MIT through fraudulent mear Furthermore, his mother was a hamster a father smelt of elderberries.

CLICK!

SENDING....

MIT 24 HOUR LIBRARY.
2:15AM.

BUMP!

134

PARKOUR! PARKOUR!

EINSTEIN SAID "IMAGINATION IS MORE IMPORTANT THAN KNOWLEDGE."

NO EXTRA CREDIT FOR AMBIANCE, SIGNORES,

HOWEVER IF YOU *DO* FINISH EARLY, PLEASE DESCRIBE AS MANY POSSIBLE WAYS TO DETERMINE THE HEIGHT OF A BUILDING USING A *BAROMETER.*

YOU WILL FIND *BOTH* ARE REQUIRED ON THIS MID-TERM.

BEGIN.

I WANT TO BE AN ASTRONAUT LIKE AN INVESTMENT BANKER WANTS HIS FIRST MILLION, HIS SECOND WIFE,

CAN I AT LEAST TAKE THE TEST AND SEE HOW I WOULD HAVE DONE?

A HOME IN THE HAMPTONS, AND ONE OF THOSE SHOE BUFFER THINGS TO PUT IN HIS CLOSET!

AS OF NOW YOU'RE STILL A STUDENT, SO I DON'T SEE WHY NOT.

BUT THEY DO HAVE A HALF-HOUR HEAD START.

SO TO RECAP... YOUR GIRL'S HATIN' ON YOU, THE FRAT'S DONE WITH YOU,

ALL YOUR STUFF IS AT THE BOTTOM OF THE RIVER, YOUR PROF KNOWS YOU FAKED YOUR WAY IN,

IS THAT THE GIST OF IT?

YEP. I'M SCREWED BECAUSE OF PRANKS ALL OVER AGAIN.

THIS LUKE GUY IS PROBABLY RATTING YOU OUT TO MIT AS WE SPEAK, PLUS YOU OWE MIT TWO GRAND BY THE END OF TODAY.

I MAY REGRET SAYING THIS, BUT IF PRANKS GOT YOU INTO ALL THIS TROUBLE...

...MAYBE *PRANKS* CAN GET YOU *OUT*. PLAY TO YOUR STRENGTHS.

I'M LISTENING.

SORRY, THAT'S ALL I GOT. YOU GOTTA FILL IN THE DEETS.

Chapter 7: Return of the Spider Closet

WHATCHA GOT THERE?

DID A NONLINEAR REGRESSION ON THE CURVES OF SHONDRA'S BOOTIE.

TURNS OUT SHE'S A FIFTH-ORDER PARABOLIC HYPERBOLOID.

I'D HIT THAT.

YOU FOLLOW THAT FIELD LINE TOPOLOGY PARADOX IN PLASMA PHYSICS TODAY?

WHAT'S NOT TO GET, DUMBASS? THE FLUX LINES RECONNECT AT THE NULL POINT.

I KNOW THAT, MOTHERFLUFFER!

DO I LOOK LIKE I'M IN NURSERY SCHOOL?

MY POINT IS THE TORUS IS A SUPERCONDUCTOR, RIGHT?

SO HOW COME THAT BASTARD DOESN'T GENERATE A DIPOLE FIELD?

RAISE THE PARTITION!

GET HIM!

WHO ARE YOU IMPERSONATING TODAY? LARRY BIRD?

CAROL, MAKE SURE THOSE GUYS ARE REALLY FROM MIT.

YOU DON'T TRUST ME?

THIS IS SO HARD.

THAT'S WHAT *SHE* SAID!

THANKS DARNELL!

CAN WE GO SOMEPLACE WHERE MY APOLOGY WON'T BE HECKLED?

PERSONALLY I DON'T CARE IF YOU GO TO MIT, CLOWN COLLEGE, OR NO COLLEGE.

BUT DO YOU HAVE ANY IDEA HOW *UNFAIR* YOUR HOAX WAS TO THIS CLINIC?

WE ONLY ACCEPT IVY LEAGUE DONORS. IF ANYONE FINDS OUT YOU FAKED YOUR WAY IN, I'LL LOSE MY JOB!

FOUR DONORS AT FIVE HUNDRED DOLLARS EACH.

I HAD NO IDEA AN MIT EDUCATION INVOLVED THIS MUCH LOCK PICKING.

JESUS, DEX, YOU LOOK *TERRIBLE!*

SLEEP DEPRIVATION HAS CONTRIBUTED TO MY HEIGHTENED STATE OF DISHEVELMENT.

STILL DOING EVERYONE'S PSETS?

IT'S PUTTING A DOWNWARD VECTOR ON MY HAPPINESS, JIM.

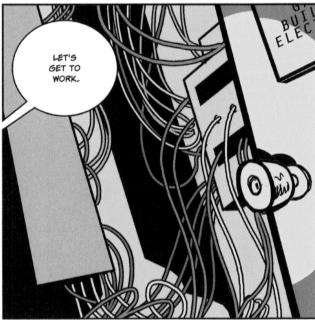

"IF HEARTY SORROW BE SUFFICIENT RANSOM FOR OFFENSE, I TENDER IT HERE."

HERE'S THE PART WHERE YOU SAY, "THEN I AM PAID...."

"...AND ONCE AGAIN I DO RECEIVE THEE HONEST."

FROM TWO GENTLEMEN OF VERONA.

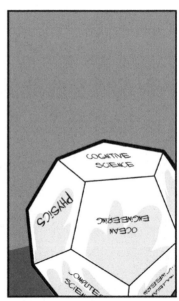

148

THAT NIGHT.

LOOKS LIKE IT'S HAPPY HOUR. COURTESY OF JIM.

149

150

PATHETIC JOB CAMOUFLAGING THAT PING-PONG BALL BLASTING TUBE.

OH, THAT WASN'T THE BLASTING TUBE. THAT WAS THE "ON" SWITCH.

CLICK. WHIRRRR

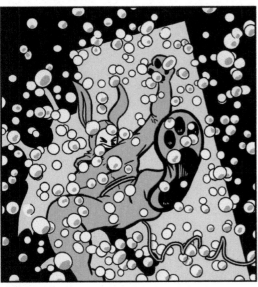

WHAT THEY DID TO MEL GIBSON AT THE END OF BRAVEHEART IS *MILD* COMPARED TO WHAT I'M GOING TO DO TO YOU!

I'M RIGHT OUTSIDE THE DOOR, LUKE. WHY DON'T YOU... *COME OUT OF THE CLOSET?*

Q.E.D., BITCH

FROM A FIGURE OF AUTHORITY TO JUST ANOTHER LUMP OF MATTER,

SUBJECT TO THE IMMUTABLE LAW OF GRAVITY.

PROFOUND.

JUST SOME WORDS OF WISDOM FROM A FRIEND.

SNAP!

SNAP!

WAIT!

I'M NOT LETTING YOU HACK ME *AND* BE THE HERO.

I'D RATHER WAIT FOR THE FREAKIN' FIRE DEPARTMENT.

LUKE, THERE'S ONLY TWO SKETCHY EYE BOLTS STANDING BETWEEN YOU AND *HALF A TON* OF HASTILY PUT-TOGETHER LUMBER.

I'LL JUST TAKE THE COSTUME OFF.

YOU *COULD*... EXCEPT YOU'RE NAKED UNDERNEATH AND WE DECORATED YOUR BODY WITH PHALLIC GRAFFITI.

TRUCE?

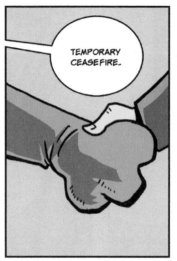

TEMPORARY CEASEFIRE.

CREAK!

FOUR DAYS LATER.

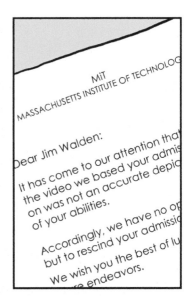

MIT
MASSACHUSETTS INSTITUTE OF TECHNOLOG

Dear Jim Walden:

It has come to our attention that
the video we based your admis
on was not an accurate depic
of your abilities.

Accordingly, we have no op
but to rescind your admissio
We wish you the best of lu
re endeavors.

YOU, THE GATEKEEPERS TO THIS ILLUSTRIOUS INSTITUTION, ARE CHARGED WITH TURNING AWAY THE UNQUALIFIED.

BUT YOU ARE NOT INFALLIBLE.

IN THE CASE OF MISTER WALDEN YOU HAVE MADE TWO *GRIEVOUS ERRORS.*

MIT ADMISSIONS COMMITTEE

MIT ADMISSIONS COMMITTEE

IN SESSION

YOUR *FIRST* WAS LETTING HIM *IN.*

YOUR *SECOND* WAS KICKING HIM *OUT.*

157

THEN IT WON'T INTEREST YOU TO KNOW THAT YOUR FRIEND DEXTER GOT A *PERFECT* SCORE.

EVEN SOLVED THE BAROMETER PROBLEM.

USE THE BAROMETER TO MEASURE AIR PRESSURE ON THE GROUND AND ON THE ROOF,

THEN CONVERT THE DIFFERENCE IN MILLIBARS TO FEET YIELDING THE HEIGHT OF THE BUILDING.

LOOKS LIKE YOU FOUND YOUR NEW LAB ASSISTANT.

YOU, ON THE OTHER HAND, GOT A *PERFECT* SCORE AND FOUND *SEVENTEEN SOLUTIONS* TO THE EXTRA CREDIT PROBLEM.

AMONG MY FAVORITES ARE "TOSS THE BAROMETER OFF THE BUILDING, TIMING ITS DESCENT TO CALCULATE HEIGHT,"

AND "TELL THE SUPERINTENDENT 'IF YOU TELL ME THE HEIGHT OF THIS BUILDING, I'LL GIVE YOU A FINE-ASS BAROMETER.' " UNORTHODOX, YET WORKABLE REAL-WORLD SOLUTIONS.

THE HIGHEST SCORE EVER. APPARENTLY YOU DO APPRECIATE THE BEAUTY OF PHYSICS...

...AMONG OTHER THINGS.

THIS MORNING I MADE AN APPEAL TO THE ADMISSIONS COMMITTEE ON YOUR BEHALF. EXPECT GOOD NEWS.

I DON'T KNOW WHAT TO SAY. THANK YOU.

YOUR PERSISTENCE MAY BECOME LEGENDARY AROUND HERE.

PROFESSOR NEUSTADT... YOU DIDN'T PULL THAT GUN ON THEM, DID YOU?

THE SUN IS ALIGNED! MIT-HENGE! IT'S HAPPENING!

SUBATOMIC PARTICLES FOR A THOUSAND.

PHYSICIST MURRAY GELL-MANN TOOK THE NAME FOR THIS PARTICLE FROM JAMES JOYCE'S FINNEGAN'S WAKE.

WHAT ARE QUARKS.

WHAT ARE NEUTRINOS?

NO. WHAT ARE QUARKS.

WHAT THE HELL?

CLASSIC ROCK FOR A THOUSAND.

THEIR 1976 SELF-TITLED DEBUT ALBUM HAS SOLD 17 MILLION COPIES.

WHAT IS BOSTON?

CORRECT!

AND THAT GIVES YOU THE LEAD WITH $4,000.

WE'LL TAKE A QUICK BREAK AND BE BACK AFTER THESE MESSAGES.

163

I LEARNED A LOT ABOUT LIFE THAT SEMESTER. EVEN HELPED CREATE SOME OF IT.

NOTES

Consult these terrific books to learn more about MIT's hacking history and culture:

Institute Historian T. F. Peterson, *Nightwork: A History of Hacks and Pranks at MIT* (MIT Press, 2011)

Samuel Jay Keyser, *Mens et Mania: The MIT Nobody Knows* (MIT Press, 2011), chapter 8, "Hacking"

Pepper White, *The Idea Factory: Learning to Think at MIT* (MIT Press, 2001), chapter 15, "Hackito Ergo Sum"

Ira Haverson and Tiffany Fulton-Pearson, *"Is This the Way to Baker House?": A Compendium of MIT Hacking Lore* (MIT Museum, 1996)

Brian M. Leibowitz, *The Journal of the Institute for Hacks, Tomfoolery & Pranks at MIT* (MIT Museum, 1990)

The following notes help separate fact from fiction and reveal a few Easter eggs. For an online version of the notes, including clickable links, visit bit.ly/geeks-notes

Chapter 1: Jim's Non-Optimal State

17   **Lord of the Fries** // Easter egg. This is a deliberate pun on William Golding's *Lord of the Flies*, a novel about a group of boys who descend into savagery when they try to govern themselves (hint, hint).

21   **Spacewar** // Easter egg. Spacewar, invented by MIT hackers in 1962, was one of the earliest video games. See bit.ly/geeks-spacewar

21   **5x5x5 Rubik's Cube** // There really is a 5×5×5 version of the Rubik's Cube, called the Professor's Cube. Incidentally, the Rubik's Cube isn't just the best-selling toy of all time. The complexity of searching for optimal Cube solving algorithms has kept top mathematicians busy for decades. See bit.ly/geeks-cube

24   **Project Searchlight** // Fiction. MIT offers scholarships based on financial need, not on any measure of merit – be it academic, athletic, artistic, or Rubik's Cube prowess. See bit.ly/geeks-aid

27   **things behind the dean's head** // Based on an actual incident I witnessed when a TV reporter was doing a stand-up in front of MIT.

27   **"hacks are to MIT what football is to Harvard"** // Easter egg. This analogy is a shout-out to one of MIT's most celebrated hacks – the legendary 1982 Harvard-Yale football game when members of MIT's Delta Kappa Epsilon fraternity rigged a weather balloon emblazoned with "MIT" to erupt from

the Harvard Stadium field at the 46-yard line. "The Harvard-Yale Football Game is MIT Hack Madness Champion," Jay London, *Slice of MIT Blog*, March 14, 2014, bit.ly/geeks-balloon

27   **KeyCab** // Easter egg. Famed architectural designer Eric Clough makes a cameo appearance in *Geeks & Greeks* as the MIT Dean. Mr. Clough has been a generous supporter of *Geeks* and many other Kickstarter projects. He and his company (212box.com) are conducting a multi-year mystery hunt called "Into Mystery," which can be found on Kickstarter and involves a series of 18 clues to, as he says, "stimulate and galvanize the multitudes." The KeyCab logo on this page is part of a final KeyAnswer.

29   **car on the dome** // Based on one of MIT's best-loved hacks (from May 9, 1994). And yes, they really did put a box of Dunkin' Donuts in the car. See *Nightwork*, p. 50-52 and bit.ly/geeks-cop-car

29   **MIT facilities workers** // Easter egg. If those MIT facilities workers remind you of MIT's most famous fictional janitor and his buddy that is purely coincidental.

30   **"police lights came from a flea market"** // Based on details revealed by the actual hackers in "A Hackers' Reunion," Stephen Eschenbach, *Technology Review*, October 2005, bit.ly/geeks-reunion

31   **"leading supplier of recreational pharmaceuticals"** // Legend has it that in the early 1970s, MIT's Bexley Hall was making about 90% of the nation's LSD supply. The FBI got wind of this and called MIT's president to alert him of an impending raid, information which he promptly shared with Bexley's housemaster. When the FBI descended on Bexley they were greeted with a "Welcome FBI" sign and painted footprints that led to a plate of milk and cookies. When the fuming agents started searching Bexley, they discovered a chest wrapped in chains and covered in padlocks. After they cut through all the chains, the agents discovered three marijuana seeds inside the chest, exactly one fewer than the minimum needed for a conviction. "Toad Sexing to a Dorm Named 'Fred': 5 Fun Facts Pulled from MIT's Hacking Stories," Lauren Landry, BostInno, bit.ly/geeks-bexley

31   **Lambda Sigma Delta shirts** // Easter egg. The fellows mixing the druggie witches brew are wearing shirts with the Greek letters Lambda Sigma Delta, an LSD reference.

31   **making the dean's door vanish** // Based on an actual hack on MIT President Charles Vest on October 15, 1990. See bit.ly/geeks-vest

32   **dry ice bomb** // Based on personal experience. The pink dye pellet is added for effect. Please do not attempt. The dangers of dry ice bombs include premature explosion which can injure the handler (burst pressure is reached in seconds), hearing damage (the explosion is extremely loud),

injury from shrapnel (the explosion propels pieces of the container), and arrest (in many jurisdictions dry ice bombs are illegal). See bit.ly/geeks-ice

33 **Golden Dome trophy** // There is no such annual award for the best hack at MIT. Like the briefcase in *Pulp Fiction*, the mineral unobtainium in *Avatar*, or the eponymous statuette in *The Maltese Falcon*, the Golden Dome trophy is a MacGuffin – a term popularized by Alfred Hitchcock for a plot device that motivates the characters and advances the story. It gives Luke a tangible goal to pursue and a reason to blackmail Jim for assistance. After all, without a heavyweight belt at stake, *Rocky* would just be two guys pummeling each other. In reality MIT students engage in hacking without prize or incentive. Now, who knows? Perhaps this graphic novel will inspire some intrepid soul to bestow an actual Golden Dome trophy. And then life will imitate art imitating life.

33 **trophy case** // Easter egg. Besides the Golden Dome trophies, AZO's trophy case also contains several Eisner Awards (the comic industry's equivalent of an Oscar), some Fields Medals (math's version of the Nobel Prize), and a hot dog eating contest trophy.

33 **rules of hacking** // The four rules of hacking in this story:
- Hacks should demonstrate wit and finesse.
- Noteworthy hacks require difficulty in execution.
- Hacks should be non-destructive.
- Don't get caught.

are my distillation of a longer set of MIT hacking ethics, which can be found at "Statement on Hacking," MIT Office of the Dean for Student Life, *The Tech*, June 13, 2008, bit.ly/geeks-hacking

33 **Tau Eta Alpha** // Easter egg. There is no Tau Eta Alpha at MIT, but the Latin alphabet equivalents of those Greek letters are THA, which stands for Technology Hackers Association, the actual MIT hacking group responsible for the cop car on the dome hack. "A Hackers' Reunion," Stephen Eschenbach, *Technology Review*, October 2005, bit.ly/geeks-reunion

33 **rappelling** // Based on actual events. My fraternity had a large contingent of students enrolled in Reserve Officer Training Corps (ROTC) programs. Ninja-like stunts and rappelling down the brownstone's exterior and interior stairwell were frequent occurrences.

34 **missing piglet prank** // Inspired by an actual 2008 high school prank in Florida. See "Billy Goats Bluff," snopes.com, bit.ly/geeks-pig

37 **Augie's silhouette** // Easter egg. As Augie emerges from the shadows the silhouette of his hair and reflection of his glasses makes him look like an owl, a visual metaphor for the role he plays in this story.

Chapter 2: The Hotel Caper

39   **"Thank you, Barton"** // Easter egg. William Barton Rogers was the founder and first president of MIT. See bit.ly/geeks-barton

41   **MILFmania.net** // Easter egg. Go ahead, visit it. You won't even have to clear your browser history.

41   **Jack Florey** // Easter egg. Jack Florey is the name of a hacking group from MIT's East Campus dormitory (Fifth East) and a well-known MIT hacker alias. See *Nightwork*, p. 207 and "Into MIT's Hidden Places: Follow the Orange Florey," Eun J. Lee, *The Tech*, August 28, 2003, bit.ly/geeks-florey

41   **"I noticed the A/C condenser was shaking so I put some shims in as a damper"** // Augie is practicing one of MIT's hacking ethics, "Always leave things as you found them, or better." See "Statement on Hacking," MIT Office of the Dean for Student Life, *The Tech*, June 13, 2008, bit.ly/geeks-hacking

41   **commandeering the hotel sign** // Based on actual events. Starting during rush week in 1967 and for many years to follow, the brothers of MIT's Alpha Tau Omega fraternity took control of the Sheraton Hotel's rooftop sign in Boston's Back Bay, turning the iconic landmark into an awe-inspiring advertisement for ATO. The method used and leverage exerted on the hotel manager in *Geeks* are fictionalized. See *Nightwork*, p. 131 and "Keyser Discusses Hacks, Culture at TBP Lecture," Jennifer Chung, *The Tech*, February 10, 1998, bit.ly/geeks-sheraton

43   ***Star Trek* trivia** // *Star Trek: The Original Series* trivia may not be the most current geek pop cultural shibboleth, but with the Gorn gag that comes later in the story, it made sense. Plus, confession time: I love William Shatner.

44   **refilling liquor bottles** // At MIT fraternities it was a common cost-saving practice to refill upscale liquor bottles with cheaper rotgut booze. *Caveat potor* ("drinker beware").

44   **Archimedes' Principle** // Archimedes' Principle states that an object immersed in a fluid is buoyed up by a force equal to the weight of the fluid it displaces. Basically it explains why ice floats.

44   **pledging a Marvin as a homework slave** // Based on actual practices at some MIT fraternities in my day.

45   **scavenger hunt** // Scavenger hunt results were routinely used to determine freshman room assignments in certain MIT fraternities.

46   **climbing the Citgo sign** // Based on actual events. Climbing the iconic Citgo sign in Kenmore Square was an exhilarating but dangerous rite of

passage when I was an MIT student. Please do not attempt. See bit.ly/geeks-citgo

46 **finish line** // This is the now sacred Boston Marathon finish line on Boylston Street.

48 **"why steal a police car"** // Of course the MIT hackers didn't actually steal a police car; they fabricated a fake one. That distinction is lost on Natalie, as it is with most people in the general public who are aware of this famous hack.

48 **"I know how to sing 'Happy Birthday' in Klingon."** // In the first 99 drafts of this script, Dexter's line was, "I know how to conjugate irregular verbs in Klingon." Then I discovered Klingon has no irregular verbs. The nerd herd would have eviscerated me for that. These are the things that keep me up at night.

51 **funnelating highly-pressurized watermelons** // Based on actual events in my misspent college years. A funnelator was an enormous slingshot made from a large plastic funnel and latex surgical tubing. See bit.ly/geeks-funnelator

53 *Busting Vegas* **book** // Easter egg. *Busting Vegas* is Ben Mezrich's follow-up book about MIT's blackjack wizards. See bit.ly/geeks-vegas

54 **painting the Smoot markers** // One of MIT's most famous hacks. Based on actual events from October 1958. See *Nightwork*, p. 142-145 and bit.ly/geeks-smoot

54 **Bridge Troll** // Inspired by an actual person. If you walked across the Harvard Bridge with any regularity in the late 1970s or early 1980s you surely noticed a peculiar man on the grassy embankment at the western foot of the bridge on the Boston side. Commonly referred to as the "Bridge Troll," this man spent his days fiercely swinging a wooden club like a caveman battling invisible enemies. The barrel-chested Bridge Troll was an imposing figure, with thick sinewy Popeye arms, strengthened from years of swinging his heavy club.

55 **"preparing to defend Earth from the invasion of the evil space reptiles from planet ten"** // Based on an actual conversation I had with said gentleman (Bridge Troll).

56 **collision ball apparatus** // Based by a real hack from 1988, although that did not include the giant paper mache Isaac Newton. See *Nightwork*, p. 158-159 and bit.ly/geeks-collision

58 **MIT football team** // The butter-fingered, turf-eating MIT football player is an anachronism, more reflective of the squad's skill during its formative

years in the late 1970s. Today MIT fields one of the best football teams in the NCAA Division III. In 2014 the Engineers went undefeated in their regular season (9-0) and won their first round playoff game. See the video at bit.ly/geeks-football

59   **85 Nobel Prize winners** // This number includes MIT's Nobel-winning alumni, faculty, and staff. For the latest stats, see bit.ly/geeks-nobel

59   **38 astronauts** // More astronauts graduated from MIT than any other non-military academic institution. For the tally as of October, 2014, see bit.ly/geeks-astro

59   **MIT cheers** // From an actual MIT cheer come the words, "Cosine, secant, tangent, sine. Three point one four one five nine." The rest of the cheers are invented. See bit.ly/mit-cheer

59   **prolate spheroid** // Technically speaking, a football is not precisely described by a prolate spheroid (the shape you get when you rotate an ellipse about its major axis), though that shape does describe a rugby ball. A football is more accurately described as a vesica piscis that has been rotated about its longitudinal axis. But the chant "Repel them! Repel them! Compel them to relinquish the vesica piscis that has been rotated about its longitudinal axis" just didn't have the right ring to it. See bit.ly/geeks-shape

Chapter 3: Thus Spake Zoltan

61   **course bibles** // Many MIT students rely heavily on course bibles – collections of questions and answers from past years' problem sets and exams. These anthologies are meticulously assembled and passed down from year to year within living groups. For a thought-provoking discussion of how the pervasive use of course bibles can mislead professors into believing that their classes are imparting knowledge as intended and even spark an "arms race" between students using bibles as a time-saving device and professors who may compensate for such shortcuts by assigning more work than can reasonably be completed, see the book *The Hidden Curriculum* by former MIT Dean of Institute Relations Benson Snyder, bit.ly/geeks-bibles

62   **chemistry problem set** // Easter egg. Chemistry geeks no doubt recognize C_2H_6O, the chemical formula for ethanol (a.k.a. drinking alcohol) on Dexter's organic chemistry problem set.

63   **blue shirt** // Easter egg. The mathematical expressions on the blue shirt translates to "i 8 sum pi," i.e. "I ate some pie."

64   **Dice of Doom** // A real thing in my fraternity. See Dice of Doom discussion in the Introduction.

65   **Dice of Doom font** // Easter egg. The Dice of Doom font is based on the handwriting of French cartoon master Jean "Moebius" Giraud. Moebius contributed storyboards and concept designs to many classic sci-fi films, including *Alien*, *The Abyss*, and *The Fifth Element*. See bit.ly/geeks-moebius

66   **Mechanical Engineering prank** // Based on an actual prank in my fraternity. Opening the hazee's bedroom door toppled dominoes, triggering various rubegoldbergian devices installed throughout the room. Springs, levers, pulleys, and rolling balls working in balletic precision resulted in catapults propelling gobs of chocolate pudding through the air onto the victim from all directions. How did the perpetrators leave the room once they set up the dominoes? Easy – they snuck out the window and clamored down the fire escape.

67   **Chemistry prank** // Inspired by an actual prank in my fraternity, although Nair hair removal lotion was used in place of fast-curing water-activated polyurethane resin.

69   **Materials Science prank** // Based on an actual prank in my fraternity. See bit.ly/geeks-foil

71   **Erlenmeyer flask** // Geek alert. Yes, Jim is giving Natalie roses in an Erlenmeyer flask.

71   **Vulcan salute** // Double geek alert. And yes, Jim is giving Natalie a Vulcan "live long and prosper" salute as he exits.

72   **hacking the audio at Bill Clinton's speech** // Inspired by an actual hack that occurred in September 1987, when MIT President Paul Gray spoke to MIT's incoming class of 1991 at the President's Convocation in Kresge Auditorium and the organ was hacked to continually interrupt him with the melody "Pop Goes the Weasel." See *Mens et Mania*, p. 96, bit.ly/geeks-weasel

72   **turning the dome into a giant breast** // Based on an actual hack from 1979. See *Nightwork*, p. 56, bit.ly/geeks-breast

72   **Apollo Lunar Module on the dome** // Based on an actual hack from May 17, 2009 where a half-scale model replica of the Apollo Lunar Module was placed on MIT's Great Dome. "Hackers Leave Lunar Lander on Dome," Michael McGraw-Herdeg, *The Tech*, June 5, 2009, bit.ly/geeks-apollo

72   *Capricorn One* // *Capricorn One* was a 1977 movie about a faked Mars landing, starring O. J. Simpson as one of the astronauts.

73   **Boston mayor** // Boston mayor Marty Walsh makes a cameo appearance as the fellow walking beside the Dean.

73   **disco ball in Lobby 7** // Inspired by an actual hack from 1996. "IHTFP Hack Gallery: Chronology," bit.ly/hacks-1996

75   **"bathing the whole corridor in a golden blaze"** // This real semiannual phenomenon is known as MIThenge in a nod to Stonehenge. See bit.ly/mit-mithenge

76   **goat wearing a CalTech shirt** // MIT and CalTech have a long-standing, good-natured hacking rivalry. See bit.ly/mit-caltech

78   **lock picking** // MIT hackers are scarily adept at lock picking. They even buy locks, practice on them, and disassemble them to see how their innards work. "A Hackers' Reunion," Stephen Eschenbach, *Technology Review*, October 2005, bit.ly/geeks-reunion

81   **"Is this the way to Baker House?"** // A classic hacker's blame-evading ruse when caught mid-hack by MIT campus police. "Hackers' Skirt Security in Late-Night MIT Treks," David Abel, *Boston Globe*, March 30, 2000, bit.ly/geeks-baker

82   **Jim falling through the skylight** // Inspired by an actual instance of a freshman falling through an MIT skylight while hacking. See the Introduction for more details. "Freshman Falls Through Bldg. 5 Skylight," Angeline Wang, *The Tech*, February 1, 2006, bit.ly/geeks-skylight

Chapter 4: Goneril and the Beaver Lover

85   **Committee on Discipline (COD) hearing** // Inspired by my actual experiences as a COD defendant and, subsequently, as a COD member.

85   **Prof. Lambeau** // Easter egg. Making a guest appearance on the COD is Prof. Lambeau, a name you may remember from *Good Will Hunting*.

86   **1841 Emerson St** // Easter egg. This fictional Cantabrigian address is a tip of the hat to Ralph Waldo Emerson and his essay "Self-Reliance," published in 1841. Emersonian notions of individualism, nonconformity, and self-reliance were very much on my mind while writing *Geeks & Greeks*. See bit.ly/geeks-emerson

87   **fertility clinic** // *Geeks* features a subplot involving a fertility clinic. Lest anyone doubt that some cash-strapped MIT students help pay tuition by moonlighting as sperm donors, let's just say there's a reason Boston-area fertility clinics have recruited donors for decades via ads in *The Tech*, MIT's student newspaper. Those ads work. I should know – I was one of those donors. See "Eggs & Sperm," Tiffany Kosolcharoen, *The Tech*, May 5, 2004, bit.ly/geeks-ads or almost any issue of *The Tech* in the last forty years, bit.ly/geeks-donors

87   **ancient magazines** // Easter egg. Natalie offers Jim a magazine from the 1950s.

90   **"High-speed stroboscopic photography"** // Easter egg. This is an homage to the late Dr. Harold "Doc" Edgerton, the MIT professor who revolutionized photography by inventing the strobe flash in the 1930s. Aside from sharing similar research interests, Prof. Neustadt is not based on Prof. Edgerton. See bit.ly/geeks-doc

90   **Green Building becomes world's largest sound meter** // Based on an actual hack from July 4, 1993. See *Nightwork*, p. 76, bit.ly/geeks-green

92   **mission statement** // Easter egg. To save you the trouble of searching for a magnifying glass, here is the full text of the fertility clinic's mission statement on the wall behind Natalie: "We pledge to do all we can to help you create the family of your dreams. And if, by chance, your baby comes out with a tail or heat vision, we swear it has nothing to do with our lab's use of mutagenic radiation. No returns, no exchanges."

93   **beaver trying to dam the Charles River** // True story and Easter egg. I once really did see a beaver attempting to dam the Charles despite the river's thousand-foot width at that point. Also MIT's official mascot is Tim the Beaver. Can you find the word "TIM" hidden in the grass in panel 3 and scratched into the log in panel 4? See bit.ly/geeks-beaver

93   **Jim and Natalie's courtship** // Inspired by actual events. Jim's geeky courting of Shakespeare-obsessed Natalie is inspired by my own bumbling pursuit of a Shakespearean actress, the woman who became my wife.

94   **"This is Goneril from *King Lear*"** // Easter egg. For many years *King Lear* was required reading in MIT's introductory humanities courses. See "The Institute Screw," bit.ly/geeks-screw

95   **Goneril's monologue** // Natalie graciously abridged Goneril's monologue slightly to fit the panel.

96   **Luke's email** // Easter egg. Luke ends his draft email with the French soldier's fatuous taunts from geek cultural touchstone *Monty Python and the Holy Grail*. See bit.ly/geeks-monty

98   **inflatable Loch Ness monster on the Charles River** // Inspired by an actual event from April 3, 1984 where a 75-foot inflatable yellow octopus was deployed on the Charles River near the MIT boathouse. Surprisingly, this was not an MIT hack, but rather a publicity stunt by a firm that rents inflatables. "Inflatable Octopus Stops Mass. Traffic," *Lewiston Journal* (Lewiston, ME), April 4, 1984, bit.ly/charles-octopus

99   **MIT Planetarium** // MIT does not currently have a planetarium, although I'm sure it will someday.

99   **moons of Uranus** // Of Uranus's 27 known moons, 24 are named after characters from Shakespeare's plays and 3 are named for characters in Alexander Pope's poem "The Rape of the Lock."

99   **Heart Nebula** // The Heart Nebula illustration is based on a photo taken by Flickr user "s58y" under Creative Commons license (CC BY 2.0). See bit.ly/geeks-nebula

Chapter 5: Ratsicle Revenge

101   **42** // Jim's score on the physics test is also "The Answer to the Ultimate Question of Life, the Universe, and Everything" according to *The Hitchhiker's Guide to the Galaxy* by Douglas Adams. See bit.ly/geeks-42

103   **exploding roach motel in desk drawer** // Based on firsthand experience. Nasty.

103   **use of drunken Bridge Troll as a bioweapon** // I'm happy to say this plot element is fictional.

104   **pink flamingos on Killian Court** // Inspired by an actual prank at the University of Wisconsin-Madison from 1979 involving a thousand plastic pink flamingos. See Neil Steinberg, *If at All Possible, Involve a Cow: The Book of College Pranks* (St. Martin's Press, 1992) and bit.ly/pink-flamingos

105   **pulling the chair away** // Prof. Neustadt's perspectives on the nature of pranks have been informed by Arthur Koestler's article on practical jokes in the *Encyclopedia Britannica*. See bit.ly/geeks-koestler

105   **Gorn** // It would be a first-order nerdcrime to mistake a reptilian humanoid Gorn from *Star Trek* for a reptilian humanoid Sleestak from *Land of the Lost*. Behold the awesomeness that is Kirk vs. Gorn bit.ly/gorn-battle

107   **red shirt** // Easter egg. Dexter's shirt color is an inside joke about the peril Dexter faces in this scene. On *Star Trek: The Original Series* red-shirted crew members had a habit of dying. Of the 59 crew members killed in the series, 43 (73%) wore a red shirt. See "Analytics According to Captain Kirk," Matt Bailey, SiteLogic, bit.ly/red-shirt-stats

111   **Halfway to Hell** // Easter egg. At the midpoint of the Harvard Bridge (which leads to MIT... don't ask) these words are painted on the sidewalk. Hell, of course, refers to MIT. See bit.ly/geeks-hell

111   **Room 273** // Easter egg. Some of you brainiacs assuredly caught the connection between the cryogenics lab being in room 273 and the fact that absolute zero is -273.15°C.

111   **ratsicles** // A real thing. This odious prank involves dipping a dead rat in liquid nitrogen until it becomes brittle, then shattering it into a thousand

pieces in a victim's room to thaw, rot, and stink. The prank is legendary at CalTech and was practiced at MIT when I was a student. See "RF" (short for Rat F*ck) at bit.ly/ratsicle

111   **"I try to avoid the MIT meal plan"** // Just kidding. MIT campus food is actually pretty decent. It earned a B+ at this rating site: bit.ly/geeks-food

113   **"What fresh hell is this?"** // Augie is quoting Dorothy Parker, who reportedly exclaimed "What fresh hell can this be?" whenever her train of thought was interrupted by the phone or a knock at the door. See bit.ly/dorothy-parker

Chapter 6: MilliHelens and Microbrews

115   **bounty for African-American sperm donors** // True story. I was offered just such a bounty by a Boston fertility clinic.

117   **"Brute force is the last resort of the incompetent."** // Dexter is quoting one of MIT's unofficial hacking guidelines. See "Statement on Hacking," MIT Office of the Dean for Student Life, *The Tech*, June 13, 2008, bit.ly/geeks-hacking

117   **Quincy Quarries** // When I was an MIT student the flooded, sheer-walled quarries were a popular spot for cliff jumping. But the treacherous waters were strewn with unseen hazards and proved lethal many times. "In Quarry's Dark Water, Grim Tales of Danger and Despair," Carey Goldberg, *New York Times*, December 7, 1997, bit.ly/quincy-quarries. Armchair meteorologists may raise an eyebrow at the gang making an autumnal cliff-jumping excursion to the quarries. Brisk swimming to be sure, but temps have hit 90° in Boston in October on occasion. This incident takes place during one such heat wave.

118   **granite** // Quincy's high-quality granite was prized for its hardness and durability. In the 19th century, Quincy's 54 quarries provided the granite to build much of Boston, including the Bunker Hill monument, Faneuil Hall, the Charlestown Navy Yard, Massachusetts General Hospital, and the Boston Custom House. See bit.ly/geeks-granite

120   **"This cliff is one hundred feet high."** // As Dexter states, the distance traveled by a falling object is $\frac{1}{2} gt^2$, where g = Earth's gravitational acceleration and t = time. Here g=32 ft/sec^2 and t=2.5 secs. $\frac{1}{2}$ (32) 2.5^2 = 100. See bit.ly/geeks-jump

121   **submerged logs at Quincy Quarries** // True story. City officials tried to discourage cliff jumping at the Quincy Quarries through various means, including pouring diesel fuel on the water and covering the surface with trees and old telephone poles. Unfortunately, these obstructions soon became waterlogged and sank just below the surface, invisible to the cliff jumpers above. The injury and fatality rate soared. See bit.ly/quincy-logs

129   **"I'm goin' Krakatoa!"** // The explosion of the Krakatoa volcano in the western Pacific Ocean in August 1883 was one of the largest eruptions in recorded history.

129   **Ocean Engineering** // MIT's Department of Ocean Engineering is no longer a stand-alone department. In 2005 it merged with the Department of Mechanical Engineering.

132   **room contents placed on a raft on the Charles** // Inspired by an actual prank from February 1985 where MIT pranksters relocated a freshman's bed, desk, and floor lamp to the middle of the frozen Charles River. See "If M.I.T. Frosh Ted Larkin Knows His Studies Cold, He Can Credit a Textbook Case of Pranksterism," *People*, February 25, 1985, bit.ly/geeks-larkin

132   **raft explosion** // Comic history lesson. Those overlapping dots emanating from the raft explosion are called "Kirby dots" or "Kirby krackle," after their creator, comics legend Jack "King" Kirby. They are often used in comics to illustrate explosions, ray gun blasts, energy pulses, and battle auras. Andy also used them with Jim's haymaker on page 111. See bit.ly/geeks-kirby

134   **student bumping Jim's chair** // Easter egg. Apparently Riverdale High School's most famous graduate went on to MIT. Who knew? See bit.ly/geeks-sugar

135   **exam becomes an Italian restaurant** // Based on an actual event from 1978 where an MIT student covered his exam table with a red checkered tablecloth and set out a plate of bread and cheese along with three bottles of wine before settling in for the test. See *Nightwork*, p. 156 and "Exam a la Carte, 1978," MIT Press, bit.ly/geeks-exam

136   **headshots on the wall** // Easter egg. Above Prof. Neustadt is a headshot of one of Hollywood's brainiest actors: MIT dropout (and Poli Sci major) James Woods. Hollywood's other notable MIT dropout is action movie star Dolph Lundgren. In 1983 Lundgren was awarded a Fulbright Scholarship to MIT but dropped out after two weeks to become Grace Jones's bodyguard, as one does. See bit.ly/geeks-actors

136   **Jim's red jacket** // Easter egg. Jim's red jacket is one of several parallels to 1955's *Rebel Without a Cause*. In that movie, another rebellious teen Jim wears a red jacket and befriends a young lady (played by an actress named Natalie). Both Jims take a social outcast under their wings. And both *Rebel* and *Geeks* feature a relationship-building scene in a planetarium and a life-and-death incident at a cliff. See bit.ly/geeks-rebel

Chapter 7: Return of the Spider Closet

140   **Jim running with the basketball** // Easter egg. Jim's posture holding the basketball is an homage to Andy Fish friend Adam West and his campy "Some days, you just can't get rid of a bomb" pier run in the 1966 *Batman* movie. See bit.ly/geeks-batman

143   **"We only accept Ivy League donors."** // Some fertility clinics really do specialize in Ivy donors. See "Sperm Banks Seeking Ivy League Deposits," Mary Jordan, *The Washington Post*, June 1, 1994, bit.ly/geeks-sperm

144   **Einstein used a $1,500 check as a bookmark then lost the book** // True story. See "Scientist and Mob Idol," Alva Johnston, *The New Yorker*, December 2, 1933, bit.ly/geeks-check

145   **PSET** // PSET is short for problem set, MIT's term for homework. See bit.ly/geeks-pset

147   **spelling with Green Building lights** // Inspired by actual events. The 9 by 17 array of windows on MIT's Green Building has been hacked to display static words and symbols many times. And on April 20, 2012 hackers transformed it into a giant, playable, multi-color game of Tetris. To my knowledge, no one has hacked the Green Building to spell words in a scrolling fashion. See "The 'Holy Grail' of Hacks," Jessica Pourian, *The Tech*, May 1, 2012, bit.ly/geeks-tetris

151   **ping-pong ball bombardment** // Homage to an actual MIT hack from 1983 when 1,600 ping-pong balls were dropped from the Lobby 7 skylight. See *Nightwork*, p. 84, bit.ly/geeks-pong

151   **"what they did to Mel Gibson at the end of *Braveheart*"**// If you haven't seen or don't remember the movie, that would be castration and disembowelment.

153   **Spider Closet relocated to the top of the dome** // Inspired by a real hack and a real prank. In September 1986 MIT's Technology Hackers Association decided to poke fun at MIT's housing shortage by constructing atop the Great Dome a 12-foot-high, 16-foot-square house. The 28 panels of "Room 10-1000" were hauled up the side of the building and secured with ropes and cables. See *Nightwork*, p. 64 and bit.ly/geeks-reunion. A second inspiration came from an actual incident in which a sleeping fraternity brother of mine was relocated – along with his bed – to the fraternity roof. Thankfully he wasn't a sleepwalker.

153   **"Q.E.D., bitch"** // Q.E.D. stands for *quod erat demonstrandum*, Latin for "what was to be demonstrated." The phrase is often used to conclude mathematical proofs. In short, it's a mathematician's way of saying, "So there."

159   **barometer problem** // For some of Jim's other creative answers to the barometer problem, see "How to Measure the Height of a Building with a Barometer," bit.ly/barometer-problem

161   **physicist Murray Gell-Mann** // Easter egg. Dr. Gell-Mann is a Nobel Prize-winning MIT alumnus (PhD, Physics, 1951).

161   **band Boston** // Easter egg. The founder, songwriter, and musical virtuoso behind Boston is Tom Scholz, a 1969 MIT grad. See bit.ly/geeks-tom

164   **children** // Easter egg. If you noticed a difference in how children were illustrated on the beginning pages compared to the final page (wild-eyed maniacs versus angelic darlings), that was intentional. It reflects an evolution in how Jim perceives children after falling in love with Natalie. Women have the power to do that. I speak from experience.

Afterword

You're a high school student considering MIT or a parent of same. Based on the preceding pages, should you be concerned?

Unequivocally not.

Yes, it's true some MIT living groups had an *Animal House* mentality in the 60s, 70s, and 80s, but that era is long past. While the playful spirit of hacking continues to thrive at MIT, many of the more abusive impulses of its living groups have toned down. Fraternities in particular have been forced to adapt to changing societal norms. The worst offenders have had their charters suspended or revoked and, across the board, a more mature attitude has taken hold. Today's MIT student is more concerned with inventing the Next Big Thing, starting a company, and changing the world than engaging in some of the more destructive hijinks recounted here.

Imagine an MIT student today finding melting rat guts splattered across his room. I expect the student would whip out his smartphone, photograph the carnage, upload it to Twitter with the hashtags #MIT #ratsicle #disgusting, tag the MIT Dean (and perhaps his own parents), then sit back and watch the whole thing go viral. The powers-that-be would swoop in and resolve the situation before the top of the hour and the long-term outlook for the culprit's student status would not be good.

While nobody here is hankering for a return to the bad old days of rampant hazing, perhaps, for MIT alumni of a certain age (old enough to remember life before social media and ubiquitous digital cameras) this book will serve as a reminder of how we handled living group problems and interpersonal conflict on our own, without administrative or parental intervention. Sometimes we solved the problem; sometimes we exacerbated it. One thing's for sure: Life was never boring.

In closing, it's worth reiterating: If you're a bright high school student who wants to be where the most creative and dynamic shapers of the future are, you should consider MIT.[11] [12] Would I send my own children there? As a geek might say... in a nanosecond.

---

11   "How MIT Became the Most Important University in the World," Chris Vogel, *Boston Magazine*, November 2012, bit.ly/mit-important
12   "MIT Maintains its Position as the Top-Ranked University Worldwide," Josie Gurney-Read, *The Telegraph*, September 15, 2015, bit.ly/mit-top

ACKNOWLEDGMENTS

The illustration of this graphic novel was financed via Kickstarter. *Geeks & Greeks* owes its existence to these genuflection-worthy backers:

AZO Founding Fathers
Brad Feld

Phil Schefter

AZO Omnipotent Rulers
Eric Clough

Doug Norton

AZO Demi-Gods
Peter Farrell	L. Patrick Gage	John Kotter
Mick Mountz	Edwin Paulson	Andrew Rallis

AZO Overlords
Susannah Kerr Adler	Haroon Alvi	Dexter Ang
Greg Bettinger	Chad Carpenter	Michael DeAddio
Richard Evans	Adi Godrej	George Michel
Frank Reynolds	Jeremy Rishel	Bud Risser
Alina Sanchez		

AZO Exalted Leaders
Steven Alexander	Rick Bahr	Pablo Bello
Cris Bera	Pegi Cladis	Michael Corfman
Daniel Dock	Robert Drescher	Sandra Fillebrown
Lorenzo Flores	Robin Diane Goldstein	Bryan Greiner
Adam Helfant	Robert Dale Klein	Robert Kurkjian
Greg Maglathlin	Thomas McKim	Ryan Morrow
Bill Mosier	Louis Nagode	Jacques Nasser
Mukta Nayak	Steve Reckitt	R. Scott Rowland
Earle Robert Shields	Brian Sparling	Voldi Way
Nick Williams		

AZO Presidents
Carol Aldrich	Morio Alexander	George Allen
Michael Beregovsky	Alexa Bettinger	Olivia Bettinger
Sara Bettinger	Eric Bogatin	Jason Huck Bradford
Michael Bruce-Lockhart	Arthur Bushkin	Peter Canepa
Al Chang	Jeff Chang	Geoff Chatterton
Michael Cleary	Martina Cochran	Craig Cohen
John Compton	Felix Dashevsky	Scott Davis
John DeTore	Tom Devlin	Austin Ellis
Joshua Ertischek	Andy Fish	Ed Forzani
Anya Freedman	James Garner	Sarah Gavit
Arthur Gleckler	Barry Gloger	Clint Grimes
Alex Gruzen	Tom Hallam	David Harrahy
James Harris	James Heywood	Ralph Inglese

Coe Ishimoto
Stephen Johnson
Jeffrey Killian
William Lange
Robert MacDonald
Jim March
Lisa Masson
Douglas McLeod
David Mitchell
Andrij Neczwid
Dan Pugh
Alex Rigopulos
Jeff Sakaguchi
Robert Schroeder
Ed Seidewitz
James Sholer
Suzanne Sophos
Sid Stookey
David Underwood
Rich White
James Yankaskas

Michael Jemiolo
Larry Kaiden
Steve Kirsch
Derek Lisinski
Bruce Main
Ed Margulies
Rick McCain
Shaun Meredith
Alfred Morgan
Stuart Olmsted
Mark Restino
Robert Sah
Mark Scher
Mary Kate Scott
George Seymour
Greg Sills
David Soule
Alex Sverdlov
Manny Voumvourakis
Greg Wilson

Eric Johns
Stephen Kelly
Steve Krueger
Jack Little
Arsen Mamikonyan
Stefanos Marnerides
Kristen McIntyre
Steeve Milliard
Mike Myers
David Powell
Susan Riedel
Suchitra Sairam
Brad Schrader
Shawn Seale
Mark Shirley
Bart Solenthaler
Eben Stiefel
Drea Pressley Tischhauser
Ken Westlund
Kelvin Pang Guo Xiang

Megathanks to the following rockstars, who graciously provided invaluable story notes, development assistance, and other material aid to this graphic novel or its primordial incarnation as a screenplay:

Dakota Aesquivel
Augie Altes
Ethan Barrett
Philippa Burgess
Felix Dashevsky
Allen Fischer
Rob Gallagher
Ken Greenblatt
Heather Juergensen
Mike Lackey
Juan Madrigal
Dan Pugh
Martin Santacruz
Jeff Thal
John Yarincik

Geoff Alexander
Remy Altes
Mike Beazel
Andrew Cannava
Thea DeSando
Myke Friscia
Dan Gebretensai
David Heyman
Joe Kelleher
Rob Lucadello
Geoff Morley
Carson Reeves
Sandra Stankovic
Marc Watrel
Dottie Zicklin

Lou Alexander
Tiffni Altes
Ralph Brescia
Steve Cartun
Matt Feitshans
Nick Fuhrman
Denise Gientke
Annalisa Hounsome
Chris Kowalczyk
Victoria Lucadello
Gregg Moscot
Marc Rosen
Julie Stern
Brooklyn Weaver
Terri Zinner

Finally, I'd like to thank the legions of MIT hackers whose imaginative and playful pranks provided the backbone for this story. The credit for any ingenuity contained herein belongs to them, not me.

Big, awkward, geeky hugs to you all.

CREATIVE TEAM

Writer **STEVE ALTES** has three degrees from MIT and worked as a rocket scientist before becoming a writer. He left engineering the day he realized two things: (1) engineering is a no-nonsense profession and (2) he is all nonsense. Plus, after your third rocket blows up, people start talking. Suddenly it might not just be the drinking.

SteveAltes.com

Artist **ANDY FISH** is an artist, writer, painter, pop culture archaeologist, and film historian. He has created numerous graphic novels and comic books and has a painting in the collection of the National Gallery of Art in Washington, DC. He is also a devourer of planets and cake, especially planets made of cake.

AndyTFish.com

Colorist **VERONICA FISH** is an artist whose paintings have been shown in galleries around the world. She's done storyboarding for film and TV and lectures on graphic novels and the history of sequential art. She has drawn for Marvel and is the lead artist for *Archie* comics.

VeronicaFish.com

For news about *Geeks & Greeks* visit:
geeks-and-greeks.com

For news about Steve Altes and Andy Fish's next graphic novel,
The Skeptic, visit:
the-skeptic.com